The Mo

Vol. 14 JOU No. 4

TEACHING

POETRY

PROPHECY

CHRONICLES

Morning Star Journal® USPS012-903 is published quarterly, 4 issues per
r, by MorningStar Publications, Inc. A division of MorningStar Fellowship
urch, P.O. Box 440, Wilkesboro, NC 28697. Fall 2004 issue. Periodicals postage
es paid at North Wilkesboro, NC and additional mailing offices. CPC
eement #1472593. ISSN# 10832122
STMASTER: Send address corrections to ***The Morning Star Journal***®,
. Box 440, Wilkesboro, NC 28697
bscription rates: One year $16.95; Outside U.S. $24.95 USD.

MorningStar Publications is a non-profit organization dedicated to the promulgation of important teachings and timely prophetic messages to the church. We also attempt to promote interchange between the different streams and denominations in the body of Christ.

To receive a subscription to ***The Morning Star Journal***®, send payment along with your name and address to *MorningStar Publications*, P.O. Box 440, Wilkesboro, NC 28697, (336) 651-2400 (1-800-542-0278—Credit Card Orders Only); fax (336) 651-2430. One year (4 quarterly issues) U.S. $16.95; Outside U.S. $24.95 USD. Prices are subject to change without notice.

BIOS

Robin McMillan is currently pastoring the MorningStar Fellowsh Church in Charlotte, North Carolina. With a unique preaching styl prophetic giftings, and a desire for the release of God's power, many a impacted by Robin's ministry. Robin and his wife, Donna, live in Nor Carolina and have four children: John Mark, Christopher, Andy, and Ka

Angie Thompson is a homeschooling mother of five great kids and t wife of Steve Thompson, author of *"You May All Prophesy"* and associa director of MorningStar Fellowship Church. She is also a writer, speaker (her schedule allows), and leader in the women's ministry at MorningSta Her vision is to encourage women to love their husbands and care for the families, while pursuing excellence and impacting the body of Christ. Ang lives in North Carolina with her husband, Steve, and their five children: Jo Josh, Madison, Moriah, and Olivia.

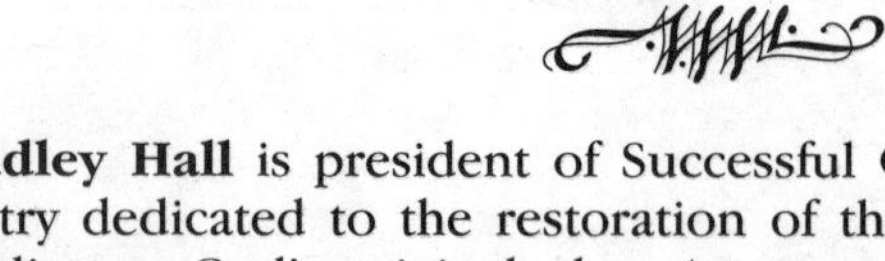

Dudley Hall is president of Successful Christian Living Ministries, ministry dedicated to the restoration of the individual and the chur according to God's original plan. As a teacher and popular conferen speaker within the body of Christ, Dudley shares the truths which God h imparted to him simply and concisely, offering practical insights to enab believers to grow in their relationships with Christ. Dudley is the author numerous books, which titles include *Grace Works, A Treasure Worth t Effort,* and *Incense and Thunder.* He and his wife, Betsy, live in Texas wi their two children: David and Karis.

Wade Taylor is the founder and former president of Pinecrest Bib Training Center in Salisbury Center, New York. He currently edits t quarterly publication, *The Banner.* He is the author of numerous trac and articles and has written two books available through MorningStar, *T Secret of the Stairs,* and *Waterspouts of Glory.* He travels extensivel ministering in churches and conferences.

Francis Frangipane is the senior pastor of River of Life Ministries Cedar Rapids, Iowa, and the president of Advancing Church Ministries. T Lord has used Francis to unite thousands of pastors in prayer in hundre of cities. With more than a million copies of his best selling books in prin and with an expanding radio and television ministry called "In Christ Image," Francis is in much demand worldwide. His newest book is entitle *It's Time to End Church Splits.*

All Scriptures are New King James Version.

by Robin McMillan

The success of our fundamental mission in this generation depends upon our proficiency in laying hold of the heavenly realm. Heaven is not just the place believers go when they die; it is God's storehouse for everything we need. Our challenges require supernatural solutions.

Heaven on Earth: Jesus' Prayer Directive

In the Lord's Prayer, Jesus taught His disciples to pray for the kingdom of heaven to come to earth.

> **"Our Father in heaven, hallowed be Your name.**
>
> **Your kingdom come. Your will be done on earth as it is in heaven.**
>
> **Give us this day our daily bread.**
>
> **And forgive us our debts, as we forgive our debtors.**
>
> **And do not lead us into temptation, but deliver us from the evil one. For Yours is the kingdom and the power and the glory forever. Amen" (Matthew 6:9-13).**

To many, this prayer has become a worship service benediction when it was intended to stimulate the church to bombard heaven for earth's needed resources. **"Your kingdom come. Your will be done on earth as it is in heaven"** is its focus. Following that proclamation comes specific agreements covering three main areas of human need that heaven can supply: daily provision, renewed relationships with God and man through giving and receiving forgiveness, and deliverance from evil. Can we be assured that God will answer this prayer? Yes, for Jesus authorized it, the kingdom, the power, and the glory is God's, and it is our Father's good pleasure to give us this kingdom (see Luke 12:32).

JUST AS DIVINE POWER SHOULD BE RELEASED IN RESPONSE TO KINGDOM ORIENTED PRAYER, SO SHOULD DIVINE DEMONSTRATIONS FOLLOW THE PROCLAMATION OF THE KINGDOM OF HEAVEN.

What Did Jesus Preach?

Jesus' preaching was as focused as His prayer life. He preached the present availability of the kingdom of heaven:

> **From that time Jesus began to preach and to say, 'Repent, for the kingdom of heaven is at hand' (Matthew 4:17).**

John the Baptist before Him (see Matthew 3:2), the original apostles with Him (see Luke 9:2), and the apostle Paul (see Acts 19:8) after Him, all preached the gospel of the kingdom of heaven. Jesus' clear instructions to all of us are found in Matthew 10:7-8:

> **"And as you go, preach, saying, 'The kingdom of heaven is at hand.'**
>
> **"Heal the sick, cleanse the lepers, raise the dead, cast out demons. Freely you have received, freely give.'"**

Just as divine power should be released in response to kingdom oriented prayer, so should divine demonstrations follow the proclamation of the kingdom of heaven. These demonstrations include healing the sick, miraculous restoration from disfiguring and deadly diseases such as leprosy, casting out demons, and even the raising of the dead.

Necessities for Heavenly Power

To operate in spiritual power, one must experience a heavenly birth and live a heavenly life. Jesus' encounter with Nicodemus addresses both issues.

The Heavenly Birth

Considered the foremost teacher in Israel, Nicodemus knew the law but had little understanding of the realm of the Spirit. Jesus explained to him the necessity of being born again, a term He used to identify a second spiritual birth whose origin was heaven and whose source was the Holy Spirit.

> **Now there was a certain man among the Pharisees named Nicodemus, a ruler (a leader, an authority) among the Jews,**
>
> **Who came to Jesus at night and said to Him, Rabbi, we know *and* are certain that You have**

> **come from God [as] a Teacher; for no one can do these signs (these wonderworks, these miracles—and produce the proofs) that You do unless God is with him.**
>
> **Jesus answered him, I assure you, most solemnly I tell you, that unless a person is born again (anew, from above), he cannot ever see (know, be acquainted with, and experience) the kingdom of God.**
>
> **Nicodemus said to Him, How can a man be born when he is old? Can he enter his mother's womb again and be born? (John 3:1-4 AMP)**

Nicodemus needed a different spiritual understanding than the one he had. Hungry for a deeper spiritual life, he risked his reputation by visiting Jesus at night to discuss His miraculous ministry.

Jesus abruptly told Nicodemus he needed to be born once more, literally born from above, to have accurate perception of the kingdom that Jesus was demonstrating. Nicodemus had no idea what Jesus was talking about.

The Heavenly Life

To further challenge the understanding of Nicodemus, Jesus spoke:

> **"No one has ascended to heaven but He who came down from heaven, that is, the Son of Man *who is in heaven*" (John 3:13).**

Jesus described Himself to Nicodemus in a highly unusual way, as the ***"Son of Man, who is in heaven!"***

On Being in Heaven

Jesus proclaimed that He not only came from heaven (referring to His conception by the Holy Spirit through Mary), but that He was **"in heaven"** even as He spoke to Nicodemus though His feet were planted firmly on planet earth.

Jesus functioned simultaneously in two different spheres. His success in the earthly realm came by living from the heavenly one. He was the Head of a new order, the kingdom of heaven, and as such He was able to successfully live a heavenly life in the face of earthly, demonic, and sensual conditions.

JESUS ABRUPTLY TOLD NICODEMUS HE NEEDED TO BE BORN ONCE MORE, LITERALLY BORN FROM ABOVE, TO HAVE ACCURATE PERCEPTION OF THE KINGDOM THAT JESUS WAS DEMONSTRATING.

Jesus' reference to Himself as the ***"Son of Man*, who is in heaven,"** as opposed to "the Son of God" who is in heaven, unfolds the idea that other men can function in the same way. If other men can be born from heaven, then they can live from there as well. This is the point Jesus made to the premier teacher of the nation of Israel.

Implications of Jesus' Heavenly Perspective

To further illustrate the truth of functioning in the earth through the power of the heavens, consider the implications of Jesus cursing the fig tree recorded in Mark 11:12-14 and 20-22:

AS ON OTHER OCCASIONS JESUS DID NOT EXPLAIN HIS ACTIONS. WE ARE LEFT TO DETERMINE FOR OURSELVES WHY HE CURSED THE FIG TREE.

Now the next day, when they had come out from Bethany, He was hungry.

And seeing from afar a fig tree having leaves, He went to see if perhaps He would find something on it. When He came to it, He found nothing but leaves, *for it was not the season for figs*.

In response Jesus said to it, "Let no one eat fruit from you ever again." And His disciples heard it.

Now in the morning, as they passed by, they saw the fig tree dried up from the roots.

And Peter, remembering, said to Him, "Rabbi, look! The fig tree which You cursed has withered away."

So Jesus answered and said to them, "Have faith in God."

Why would Jesus curse the fig tree for not doing what it could not do? The text clearly states that it was not time for figs to be on the tree, so how could He expect the tree to have them?

Poor Israel

As on other occasions Jesus did not explain His actions. We are left to determine for ourselves why He cursed the fig tree. Many have concluded that Jesus cursed the fig tree as though it represented Israel, and the cursing of Levitical Judaism for its failure to bear the fruit God expected of it. That may be a true interpretation of these verses, but surely Jesus had other more positive and redemptive reasons.

A Tree of a Higher Order

First we must recognize that Jesus was familiar with another class of tree, a heavenly one.

And he showed me a pure river of water of life, clear as crystal, proceeding from the throne of God and of the Lamb.

In the middle of its street, and on either side of the river, was the tree of life, which bore twelve fruits, each tree yielding its fruit every month. The leaves of the tree were for the healing of the nations (Revelation 22:1-2).

The kind of tree that Jesus preferred was heavenly in nature, one that bore twelve kinds of fruit each month. Unlike that pitiful, natural fig tree struggling to produce its little seasonal crop of figs just outside of Bethany, this tree is always in season, always bearing ripe fruit of supernatural varieties as well.

This tree was so potent that its leaves had supernatural properties. Leaves of certain plants in nature have limited healing properties but these leaves could heal entire nations, and restore them to the plan of God. This is the Tree of Life.

The river of water of life feeds the Tree of Life and flows from the very throne of God (see Revelation 22:1). Only that supernatural life-giving river could cause a tree to bear such remarkable and consistent fruit.

Emphasizing the Curse

Another reason Jesus cursed the fig tree was to emphasize that it was cursed already. The fig tree represented fallen humanity, never measuring up on its own when under divine scrutiny. Over and again mankind depends on the flesh to do what it is incapable of. Jesus contrasted the flesh to the Spirit in John 6:63:

> **"It is the Spirit who gives life; the flesh profits nothing. The words that I speak to you are spirit, and they are life."**

We must stop trusting in the flesh to accomplish the purposes of God. Trusting in it is a serious departure from the Lord and only ends in barrenness:

> **"Thus says the Lord, 'Cursed is the man who trusts in man and makes flesh his strength, whose heart departs from the LORD.**
>
> **For he shall be like a shrub in the desert, and shall not see when good comes, but shall inhabit the parched places in the wilderness, in a salt land which is not inhabited" (Jeremiah 17:5-6).**

THE KIND OF TREE THAT JESUS PREFERRED WAS HEAVENLY IN NATURE, ONE THAT BORE TWELVE KINDS OF FRUIT EACH MONTH.

The flesh can never accomplish what the Spirit can. When Jesus first approached the tree it was because He was hungry. Obviously this hunger of Jesus' was a natural one, but it speaks of a hunger that cannot be filled by something less than Spirit and life. Depending on that tree would never satisfy the deepest hunger of the Son of Man and it will not satisfy ours either.

Emphasizing Normalcy

The church lives at such a low level of spiritual life today that our idea of normal is inaccurate. Jesus was the only normal Man the world has seen. He showed us how a man can live who is filled with the Holy Spirit and in communion with God the Father. His act of cursing the fruitless fig tree was an action commentary on what He knew normal fruit bearing to be.

EVERYTHING WE WILL EVER NEED HAS ALREADY BEEN CREATED FOR US AND IS STORED IN HEAVEN, WAITING FOR US TO EXERCISE FAITH TO RECEIVE IT OR ACTIVATE IT FOR OTHERS.

Are the Tree and River Available Now?

It is clear that Jesus operated from heaven at the highest level, but what can you and I do? Is it true that the resources of heaven are available to us? To address this question let us first consider several of Paul's revelatory statements from the book of Ephesians:

> **"Blessed be the God and Father of our Lord Jesus Christ, who has blessed us with every spiritual blessing in the heavenly places in Christ..." (Ephesians 1:3).**

> **"and raised us up together, and made us sit together in the heavenly places in Christ Jesus..." (Ephesians 2:6).**

> **"For we are His workmanship, created in Christ Jesus for good works, which God prepared beforehand that we should walk in them" (Ephesians 2:10).**

Several facts are made clear from Paul's writings:

- Every spiritual blessing we will ever need is presently available.
- God has already created them for us.
- They are located in heaven and are in Christ Jesus.
- God has made us sit in the same place with Christ and these blessings.

In no uncertain terms the apostle Paul describes our limitless wealth in Christ Jesus. Everything we will ever need has already been created for us and is stored in heaven, waiting for us to exercise faith to receive it or activate it for others. If we can but learn to live out of that place, we will consistently access the wealth of heaven.

The River of Life and the Tree of Life

Consider once again the passage from Revelation 22 describing the river and the tree:

> **"And he showed me a pure river of water of life, clear as crystal, proceeding from the throne of God and of the Lamb.**
>
> **In the middle of its street, and on either side of the river, was the tree of life, which bore twelve fruits, each tree yielding its fruit every month. And the leaves of the tree were**

for the healing of the nations" (Revelation 22:1-2).

How can we know that we have access to both the river and the Tree of Life? The Bible tells us so. In Revelation 22:17 we read:

> **"And the Spirit and the bride say, "Come!" And let him who hears say, "Come!" And let him who thirsts come. Whoever desires, let him take the water of life freely."**

Jesus offered supernatural water to people on numerous occasions. He promised it to the woman with five husbands at Jacob's well (see John 4:14) and He promised it to the multitude in the temple during His last feast of Tabernacles (see John 6:35). God has invited us to come and drink freely from the water of life.

Concerning the tree of life, consider the language describing it. It bears twelve kinds of fruit each month and its leaves are for the healing of the nations. We must remember that there are no months in heaven. Days, nights, weeks, months, and seasons all correspond to life on earth. These increments of time are related to the rotation of the earth and its proximity to the sun. In heaven there is no sun and no nighttime, therefore there are no seasons. **"The city had no need of the sun or of the moon to shine in it, for the glory of God illuminated it. The Lamb is its light" (Revelation 21:23).**

Yes, Jesus Christ Himself is the Light of the place called heaven. The language used to describe the tree of life in the terms of seasons and months is poetic/prophetic language, to help us understand that these things are available for us right now in time.

Think also about the leaves of the tree being for the healing of the nations. The nations will not need healing in heaven but they need healing right now. As ambassadors of the kingdom of heaven we can obtain by faith the substance of these healing leaves and release their healing power.

THE LANGUAGE USED TO DESCRIBE THE TREE OF LIFE IN THE TERMS OF SEASONS AND MONTHS IS POETIC/ PROPHETIC LANGUAGE, TO HELP US UNDERSTAND THAT THESE THINGS ARE AVAILABLE FOR US RIGHT NOW IN TIME.

Called to Bear Fruit

Bearing fruit has always been a high priority with God. In the beginning God created a garden and made it Adam's first home. Part of his calling and responsibility was to tend and cultivate that garden (see Genesis 2:15). You and I have gardens as well, but our gardens are spiritual ones. We have been called to produce supernatural fruit. The only way we can do so is to abide in Jesus, the vine:

> **"I am the true vine, and My Father is the vinedresser.**
>
> **"Abide in Me, and I in you. As the branch cannot bear fruit of itself, unless it abides in the**

vine, neither can you, unless you abide in Me.

"I am the vine, you are the branches. He who abides in Me, and I in him, bears much fruit; for without Me you can do nothing.

> MOST OF OUR LIVES DO NOT MEASURE UP TO JESUS' EXPECTATION BECAUSE WE HAVE NOT HAD A SUFFICIENTLY *VIOLENT* APPROACH TO THE KINGDOM OF HEAVEN.

"If you abide in Me, and My words abide in you, you will ask what you desire, and it shall be done for you.

"By this My Father is glorified, that you bear much fruit; so you will be My disciples" (John 15:1, 4-5, 7-8).

The Tree of Life and its fruit speak of what is available to us as we abide in Christ, seated with Him in the heavenly places. Jesus makes this remarkable promise to all who do, **"If you abide in Me, and My words abide in you, you will ask what you desire, and it shall be done for you."** That is a kingdom promise of the highest order. The Tree of Life and the river of life are available to us even now.

Conclusion

Jesus describes how our lives should be lived as He identifies the greatness of John the Baptist and compares him to a standard issue saint in the kingdom of heaven:

"Assuredly, I say to you, among those born of women there has not risen one greater than John the Baptist; but he who is least in the kingdom of heaven is greater than he.

And from the days of John the Baptist until now the kingdom of heaven suffers violence, and the violent take it by force" (Matthew 11:11-12).

Most of our lives do not measure up to Jesus' expectation because we have not had a sufficiently *violent* approach to the kingdom of heaven. The Amplified translation of this verse gives us more insight into how we may experience the blessings of the kingdom:

"And from the days of John the Baptist until the present time, the kingdom of heaven has endured violent assault, and violent men seize it by force" [as a precious prize—a share in the heavenly kingdom is sought with most ardent zeal and intense exertion] (Matthew 11:12 AMP).

Our lives must be lived as kingdom people. We shall not inherit that great kingdom by living quiet lives of self-satisfied complacency. We must take it by force and we must take it now. ■

The power of Being in your Place

by Angie Thompson

In Western society, fame, power, and position are highly valued. These attributes can also be useful for influence in the kingdom. In the same way, visibility *can* be a pathway to influence. But there are many men and women in God's kingdom who are dedicating the majority of their time to provide for and build their families. Without question, this ministry to our families is of primary importance to God. I Timothy 3 addresses this, as does I Timothy 5:8: **"But if anyone does not provide for his own, and especially for those of his household, he has denied the faith, and is worse than an unbeliever."** However, for any who are seemingly invisible, temptation can arise to make one feel insignificant in the bigger picture of ministry. Many begin to feel that they are "stuck at home" or "stuck in a job" and that they could be much more effective if they were free to pursue ministry in the traditional venues (minus the responsibilities of home life).

In our quest for significance in God's plan, it is important to realize that God's values are very often different from our own. He often uses the weak and inferior as His chosen vessels. From the Scriptures, we can also see that God uses both kinds of ministries—the visible and the invisible, and that each is extremely important in fulfilling His plan.

In Judges 4, we find two examples of women who honored God and were used by Him in very different circumstances. Deborah and Jael were two women who lived diverse lives. Yet in their obedience to God in their given situations, they both played a vital role in releasing others from bondage and conquering the enemy in their midst. They were faithful to God in their unique stations in life.

Deborah, the Leader

During this time in Israel's history, the Israelites would turn away from God and, in turn, fall into the hands of their enemies. **"Then the Lord raised up judges who delivered them from the hands of those who plundered them" (Judges 2:16).** During the life of the judge, the Lord was with the judge and would deliver the Israelites from their enemies. Deborah was the judge who had been raised up at this time. She was in a significant, visible, leadership position. It says **"the sons of Israel came up to her for judgment" (Judges 4:5).**

Not only was Deborah a judge, she was also a prophetess. She provided justice and the Word of the Lord. Deborah was also the wife of Lappidoth. So, in addition to her roles of leadership, she also kept and maintained a marriage and a home. In our modern day society, we could liken her to a visible leader in the church.

When the Israelites sinned this time, they were sold into the hands of Jabin, the Canaanite king. They were oppressed and cried out to the Lord. God's response was to give Deborah a word for Barak who was to lead the armies to victory. When she summoned him and told him of God's plan, Barak's response was **"If you will go with me, then I will go; but if you will not go with me, I will not go" (Judges 4:8).** Even though God's Word was true, Barak still needed the help and assurance of having a prophet of God along with him.

As we will see later in this Scripture, the ultimate victory in the battle came not solely through Deborah, the visible leader, but through another hidden woman.

In Judges 4:9, Deborah says to Barak, **"... the honor shall *not* be yours on the journey that you are about to take, for the Lord will sell Sisera into *the hands of a woman.*"** Barak must have thought that Deborah was speaking of herself since she was a woman and she would be helping to lead the army. Perhaps even Deborah thought that the credit of the victory would be hers. We do not really know what either of them thought at the time. We only know that God was speaking prophetically about deliverance coming through the hands of a woman. As we will see later in this Scripture, the ultimate victory in the battle came not solely through Deborah, the visible leader, but through another hidden woman.

The Leader Will Continue

As the battle continued, Deborah and Barak routed the army of Sisera, the Canaanite commander. All the army of Sisera fell by the sword except for one. Sisera, their leader, escaped.

When studying history, I have come to realize that any great leader deprived of his army will eventually muster another to take its place. He can again rise to power with an army behind him. Perhaps this is why it is so important that leaders of cruel or harsh regimes be captured. Even though Hitler's armies were defeated, it was important to stop the man himself. Saddam Hussein needed to be captured in Iraq. Given time, these and other leaders may have tried to regain power and form another, more powerful army. An effective leader will learn from his mistakes and become more powerful after a defeat. This is probably what would have happened with Sisera. He would have retreated for a while but come back with more men and a better plan to defeat the Israelites the next time.

Jael, Hidden in Her Tent

When Sisera fled, he came to the tent of Jael. Previous to this point, we have never heard of Jael and know nothing about her. The Scriptures say that she was in her tent. She was hidden. She was probably taking care of her family and responsibilities at home. She was not on the battlefield in a visible ministry, and not even part of the Israelite camp. She was a Midianite, a descendant of Abraham through his wife Keturah (see Genesis 25:1-2), but not a descendant of Isaac. She was of the line of Moses' father-in-law, Jethro. So even though Jael was not in the Israelite camp, she knew of God, His traditions, and His commandments. God had a purpose for her life, and she was a willing servant in that purpose.

So even though Jael was not in the Israelite camp, she knew of God, His traditions, and His commandments. God had a purpose for her life, and she was a willing servant in that purpose.

When Sisera came to her tent, Jael came out to meet him. She must have known of the battle, for she was looking for him. She earned his trust by saying, **"...Turn aside to me! Do not be afraid" (Judges 4:18).** She covered him with a rug. He asked for water and she strategically gave him milk. Knowing he was weary from battle, she did what she could to put him to sleep. She was not merely opportunistic, but was planning from the time he entered her tent to kill him. Even though she was not a warrior on the battlefield, she had a warrior-mentality.

She was a warrior in her heart, and she was prepared when the opportunity came.

While the enemy was unaware and sleeping, she quietly took a tent peg and a hammer in her hands. Tent pegs were stakes, probably wooden ones, that were used in the setting up and holding up their tents. This stake represented Jael's life—building the foundation of her home. She knew how to use it because she used it often. According to tradition, the Midianites were gypsies. She had been faithful in taking down her tent and putting it up again each time she moved. In the hands of a servant of God, a tool for building became a weapon to overcome the enemy!

The final victory in this battle came as Jael drove the stake into the temple of the enemy leader's head and put him to death. She struck with a quick and severe blow. What strength! What obedience—from a common, hidden person! When the Israelites entered the camp, Jael went out to meet Barak to show him the victory. In verse 22, she says **"Come, and I will show you the man whom you are seeking."** We see in the verses following that **"God subdued on that day Jabin the king of Canaan before the sons of Israel. And the hand of the sons of Israel pressed heavier and heavier upon Jabin the king of Canaan, until they had destroyed Jabin the king of Canaan" (Judges 4:23-24).** It was this victory that led the sons of Israel into ultimate deliverance from their enemy and oppressor—the Canaanite king!

> It was this victory that led the sons of Israel into ultimate deliverance from their enemy and oppressor—the Canaanite king!

What is Your Place?

As we see so clearly in this passage, strength and power come from knowing our place and being in that place when God calls. There are those who have a visible place of leadership. Without the leadership of Deborah, the Israelites would not have even gone to battle against their enemy. It was through her obedience and leadership that the enemy army was destroyed. We must have strong leaders who are willing not only to bring a word of truth and deliverance, but also those who are willing to go forth and lead to the fulfillment of the prophecy!

We need those who are content to be in the hidden places of their tents, strategically placed in diverse places, so that the Lord can route the enemy unaware into their hands. Deborah is commonly understood to be the main heroine in this story. But in Judges 5 when Deborah and Barak sing the song of victory, Jael is also given credit. **"Most blessed of women is Jael, the wife of Heber the Kenite. Most blessed is she of women in the tent" (Judges 5:24).** The verses that follow go on to recount her part in the victory over the enemy.

If we are submitted to Him and at peace in the place He has put us, we will be in a ready position when the time comes. We must constantly remember that we are in a battle. It is important that we are continually in a state of preparation for battle, even when we are not on the front line. We must not waste time by waiting to be called to the front. God will honor our faith and our faithfulness. Faithfulness is a requirement, and it is irrespective of our position.

It is true that our place can change over time. Different seasons of life bring different responsibilities and different positions. Our ultimate goal is to pursue the Lord, seeking His heart and mind, so that we will know how to act when an opportunity comes to us. Our hearts and our hands will be prepared for whatever may come our way, and we will be used to release our lives and the lives of those around us from the bondage of the enemy.

Just as God asked Moses **"What is that in your hand?" (Exodus 4:2)** and later used that staff for His purposes, we must see what it is that God has given to each of us. We must look to see what is in our hands. Deborah had influence in her hand. We could say that the leader of the army was in her hand because she had a voice with him. God gave her this position and this authority, and she was faithful with it. Jael had a tent peg in her hand. Though she was "stuck at home," she realized that she had influence. Because of her obedience, Sisera ended up being "stuck" or "struck" at home as well! Jael struck him with her tent peg in her tent. She was faithful and courageous in her position.

Our hearts and our hands will be prepared for whatever may come our way, and we will be used to release our lives and the lives of those around us from the bondage of the enemy.

With the tools in our hands, we must be aggressive in pursuing God's purposes. We must see ourselves and our positions, whether great or small, from God's perspective. There we will find power and victory, and we can be ready and useful when the opportunity comes. ■

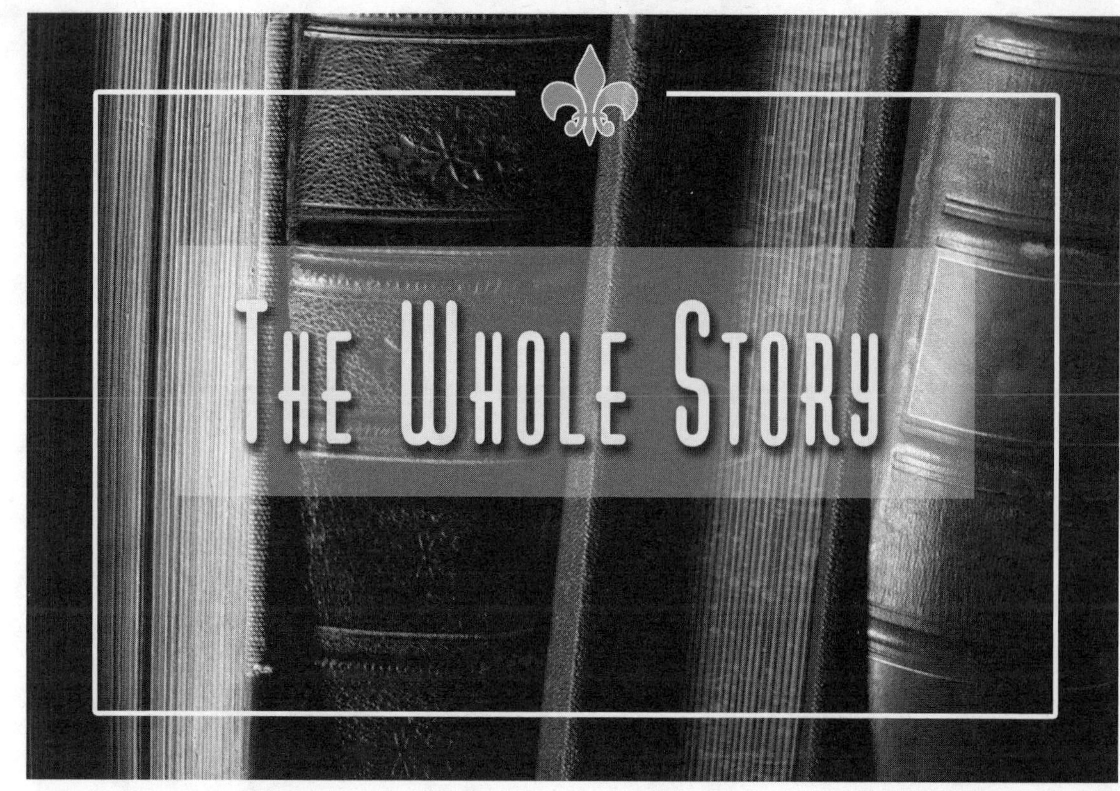

The Whole Story

by Dudley Hall

Any honest reading of the New Testament reveals a gospel that provokes controversy. Though Jesus spent His public ministry healing those who were sick, liberating people oppressed by demons, and teaching about the kingdom of God, He threatened enough of the wrong people that they had Him killed. Yet most people today do not think of Jesus as controversial. When He handed His disciples the task of proclaiming the same kingdom, most of the original twelve ended their lives as martyrs. I wonder why the Christians I know do not stir up the same hostility. It seems unlikely that our society is so aligned with God's purpose that we can preach the same gospel they did and expect to be popular and congratulated.

Jesus and the first apostles preached a gospel that motivated people to abandon one way of life and adopt another. They gladly gave up vocations, cashed in retirement plans, and forsook all forms of security. When authorities beat them for proclaiming their message, they considered it a joyful privilege. Our gospel seems so domesticated that we cannot even get people's attention, much less challenge their whole way of life. By subtracting the elements of the message that might have had us beaten, we have also stripped it of its power to change lives. The result is that we command people to quit sinning without offering them the divine power to do so. Homosexuals are supposed to go straight and addicts are supposed to go to meetings. We tell the sick there will be power to heal them when revival comes, the hungry that they will be satisfied when Jesus returns, and those burdened with sin that things will be different during the Millennium.

For God's people to make any progress, the gospel we believe and proclaim will be different than what we have usually heard and more like what is in the New Testament. The only explanation for our inadequate behavior is our faulty beliefs and it is impossible to change behavior without changing convictions. If we want to grasp more, we must be ready to let go of some of what we value now. John Wimber told a story of one pastor who was being stretched by what he was seeing of God's power to touch, heal, and liberate people. He asked, "How far is all this going to go?" and John answered him, "As far as the Bible does." For some reason that seemed to comfort this pastor, but I'm not sure why. The Bible portrays God working in ways far beyond the comfort zone for most of us. Philip was transported immediately from one place to another; Peter saw a vision that completely changed the definition of who was acceptable to God; Elijah was taken up to heaven without dying.

The gospel only makes sense as a story, a story as big as the purpose of God. It has become fashionable to talk about groups and their stories. We hear that various ethnic groups in the United States, for instance, have different stories concerning what it means to be an American. This is one of the ways that the influence of postmodern thinking is affecting us without our being aware of the scholarly debates. The era of modernism put so much emphasis on discovering universal truth through reason and the scientific method and the resulting technology that there is now a backlash against unquestioned confidence in such thinking. Modernism's story of progress based on objective and scientific knowledge proved inadequate to account for some parts of human experience, so people began to doubt the validity of any "big" story. Instead there were posited numerous "little" stories, each equally valid and deserving of the respect and tolerance of those identifying with other stories.

THE ONLY EXPLANATION FOR OUR INADEQUATE BEHAVIOR IS OUR FAULTY BELIEFS AND IT IS IMPOSSIBLE TO CHANGE BEHAVIOR WITHOUT CHANGING CONVICTIONS.

This kind of thinking is now the default philosophical basis for our lives. It controls television, popular music, and the movies. Most appalling, though, is that it also taints much of the preaching we hear. Each Christian has an individual arrangement with God, it's "just between Jesus and me." But this is not true to the New Testament account of the gospel. There is a story that explains everything, and that story is epitomized in the message of Jesus Christ. I have stood at the graveside with friends as we buried their young adult children who had taken their own lives. I know of other young people who failed in attempts to take their own lives. They had no sense of purpose and no hope worth living for. Many parents are stunned and dismayed that their kids feel this way, but so many parents themselves have little purpose to their lives. They are born, go to school, and build a career so they can retire, play golf, and eventually die. Along the way they manage to give some time and money to their church.

MANY PARENTS ARE STUNNED AND DISMAYED THAT THEIR KIDS FEEL THIS WAY, BUT SO MANY PARENTS THEMSELVES HAVE LITTLE PURPOSE TO THEIR LIVES.

The **"book of life"** in which are written the names of God's people may be very different than we have thought. Instead of being a ledger with an accounting of our good and bad behavior, perhaps it is a history. Our names are not simply listed there with our balances alongside, but they are included as characters in the great story God is creating through His people because of His Son. The gospel invites us today to join in the same story as Abraham, Esther, Paul, and Lydia. Acts 13 contains the account of one of the many times Paul proclaimed the big story of the gospel.

And Paul stood up, and motioning with his hand, he said, "Men of Israel, and you who fear God, listen:

"The God of this people Israel chose our fathers, and made the people great during their stay in the land of Egypt, and with an uplifted arm He led them out from it.

"And for a period of about forty years He put up with them in the wilderness.

"And when He had destroyed seven nations in the land of Canaan, He distributed their land as an inheritance—all of which took about four hundred and fifty years.

"And after these things He gave them judges until Samuel the prophet.

"And then they asked for a king, and God gave them Saul the son of Kish, a man of the tribe of Benjamin, for forty years.

"And after He had removed him, He raised up David to be their king, concerning whom He also testified and said, 'I have found David the son of Jesse, a man after My heart, who will do all My will.'

"From the offspring of this man, according to promise, God has brought to Israel a Savior, Jesus,

after John had proclaimed before His coming a baptism of repentance to all the people of Israel.

"And while John was completing his course, he kept saying, 'What do you suppose that I am? I am not He. But behold, one is coming after me the sandals of whose feet I am not worthy to untie'" (Acts 13:16-25).

The Gospel Is the Fulfillment of God's Plan

It is hard to read this without concluding that Paul considered God the main character in the story. Yet we often manage to read and explain the Scriptures without reference to God's role. In my boyhood Sunday school class we read the story of David and Goliath as if the hero of the story was David, the shepherd boy whose courage and faith in God gave him victory against all odds. But the hero of that story is God, not David. We also read the story about Abraham lying to Pharaoh, saying that his wife was his sister. The teacher told us we should not lie, but that never made much sense because Abraham ended up rich and blessed. It looked like lying worked out pretty well for him. But the problem is that the Bible is not a book of moralistic examples or principles for securing divine blessing. It is the story of God at work on earth.

The story of Jesus only makes sense as part of a much bigger story. God created out of love a male and a female, Adam and Eve, to become His obedient partners in the rest of His creation, but they chose independence from Him and separation. Much later, God addressed the problem of that separation by choosing a man, Abram, from the many descendants of Adam. This man would be the one through whose seed God would offer to all mankind the same kind of relationship He had intended and very briefly had with Adam and Eve. The nation that came from Abram (later called Abraham) was given God's Law so that all humanity could learn from Israel's example that knowing what is right does not empower sinful people to do what is right. But from that nation came Jesus, the ultimate descendant of Abraham, who obeyed every jot and tittle of that Law, then died to redeem those who could not. He was then resurrected and exalted so that He sent the Holy Spirit to bless all the nations with the blessing promised to Abraham.

> BUT THE PROBLEM IS THAT THE BIBLE IS NOT A BOOK OF MORALISTIC EXAMPLES OR PRINCIPLES FOR SECURING DIVINE BLESSING. IT IS THE STORY OF GOD AT WORK ON EARTH.

God was so intent on His plan being accomplished that even Israel's rejection of her promised Messiah ended up furthering rather than frustrating the plan. For Jesus to die innocently, someone had to kill Him, and Israel's rejection played its part. This is the basis for Paul's confidence in Romans 8:28 that **"all things to work together for good."** God has not dumped us into history and required us to figure things out on our own. He has a script and He invites us to become actors in the drama. Instead of finding our own way in the world, He calls us to find our way into His story.

> But we no longer wait for fulfillment because the goodness of God has been personified in Jesus Christ.

"Brethren, sons of Abraham's family, and those among you who fear God, to us the word of this salvation is sent out.

"For those who live in Jerusalem, and their rulers, recognizing neither Him nor the utterances of the prophets which are read every Sabbath, fulfilled these by condemning Him.

"And though they found no ground for putting Him to death, they asked Pilate that He be executed.

"And when they had carried out all that was written concerning Him, they took Him down from the cross and laid Him in a tomb.

"But God raised Him from the dead;

and for many days He appeared to those who came up with Him from Galilee to Jerusalem, the very ones who are now His witnesses to the people.

"And we preach to you the good news of the promise made to the fathers,

that God has fulfilled this promise to our children in that He raised up Jesus, as it is also written in the second Psalm,' Thou art My Son; today I have begotten Thee'" (Acts 13:26-33).

The Gospel Is Fulfillment in a Person

Throughout the Old Testament, God gave His people promises on which they based their hope for the future. In the New Testament those hopes are fulfilled and promises kept in Jesus Christ. No sooner had Adam and Eve sinned than God was promising Eve that her seed would overcome in the battle with the seed of the serpent. And throughout His dealings with His covenant partners, God expanded on that promise. But we no longer wait for fulfillment because the goodness of God has been personified in Jesus Christ. Things will never be better than they are in Him, and He's here with us now.

Our stance is not waiting for God to do something newer and better, but cooperating with Him in what He has already done in Christ. Instead of expecting most things to be fulfilled when Jesus returns, we should be living in the fulfillment He has already accomplished. Though it will be glorious, nothing in Jesus' last coming will compare to what He has already done. The climax of God's story has already happened, though we still expect a final consummation. Jesus Christ is the Star of God's show, and He does not share top billing with anyone or anything, not Israel or America, not preaching or small groups or movements. The focus of God's message is the person of Jesus Christ.

The Gospel Is the Fulfillment of Promises

Any divine promise you can think of has its completion in Christ. God promised Abraham that his seed would bless the world, and Jesus fulfilled that promise. He promised His people they would live in the land He had promised Abraham, and that place of rest and blessing has been expanded and fulfilled; the whole earth has become the land of promise. He promised His presence in the place of worship, but Jesus has made it so that we do not have to go anywhere in particular to meet with God.

God promised a king to sit forever on David's throne, and Jesus is that King. When people asked on the day of Pentecost what was going on, Peter answered by referring to the promise in Joel 2 and told them **"this is that," (Acts 2:16 KJV)** the last days of God's presence and power in His people. Ever since, we have lived in the blessings of last days.

Even the promise of Jesus' return is not the ultimate hope because Jesus told His disciples that it would be to their advantage for Him to depart physically and send the Holy Spirit to them (see John 16:7). No matter which box we choose to contain God, He breaks out of it. He lives in His people everywhere. Instead of reading the daily newspaper to look for what God is doing with Israel, we should be looking for what He is doing in and through His church throughout the world.

HE PROMISED HIS PRESENCE IN THE PLACE OF WORSHIP, BUT JESUS HAS MADE IT SO THAT WE DO NOT HAVE TO GO ANYWHERE IN PARTICULAR TO MEET WITH GOD.

The Gospel Offers Fulfillment to People

The best thing about God's story is that it offers a role for all who accept His invitation to participate in it by faith. When God was ready to make major changes on earth, He approached a man named Noah. He did not invite Noah to die and come to heaven, but to become a part of the story on earth that would climax with His Son. Like Noah, each of us has been found and invited by God to play a role in His redemptive agenda for man and earth. Our part is as important as Noah's, but few of us believe it.

Recent research showed that 86 percent of young people who have grown up in church youth programs drop out of church in their college years, returning to church, if at all, ten years later. They have been taken to church by their parents and taught by their example to expect to evaluate a service by how it makes them feel. They read the Bible for practical advice on daily problems and they pray for comfort and blessing. The only religion they know is centered on themselves. By the time they are in college they realize they are not getting much out of church and no one is making them go any more. They never got the message that there is a part for them to play in God's story.

BY THE TIME THEY ARE IN COLLEGE THEY REALIZE THEY ARE NOT GETTING MUCH OUT OF CHURCH AND NO ONE IS MAKING THEM GO ANY MORE.

"Therefore let it be known to you, brethren, that through Him forgiveness of sins is proclaimed to you,

and through Him everyone who believes is freed from all things, from which you could not be freed through the Law of Moses.

"Take heed therefore, so that the thing spoken of in the Prophets may not come upon you:

'Behold, you scoffers, and marvel, and perish; for I am accomplishing a work in your days, a work which you will never believe, though someone should describe it to you.' "

And as Paul and Barnabas were going out, the people kept begging that these things might be spoken to them the next Sabbath.

Now when the meeting of the synagogue had broken up, many of the Jews and of the God-fearing proselytes followed Paul and Barnabas, who, speaking to them, were urging them to continue in the grace of God.

And the next Sabbath nearly the whole city assembled to hear the word of God.

But when the Jews saw the crowds, they were filled with jealousy, and began contradicting the things spoken by Paul, and were blaspheming.

And Paul and Barnabas spoke out boldly and said, "It was necessary that the word of God should be spoken to you first; since you repudiate it, and judge yourselves unworthy of eternal life, behold, we are turning to the Gentiles.

"For thus the Lord has commanded us, 'I have placed You as a light for the Gentiles, that You should bring salvation to the end of the earth.'"

And when the Gentiles heard this, they began rejoicing and glorifying the word of the Lord; and

as many as had been appointed to eternal life believed.

And the word of the Lord was being spread through the whole region.

But the Jews aroused the devout women of prominence and the leading men of the city, and instigated a persecution against Paul and Barnabas, and drove them out of their district.

But they shook off the dust of their feet in protest against them and went to Iconium.

And the disciples were continually filled with joy and with the Holy Spirit (Acts 13:38-52).

We cannot be surprised when people scoff at hearing us proclaim a gospel as audacious as this. Just as Israel could not believe that God would send a foreign power to destroy them, people cannot fathom the implications of such a story as the one we have to tell. But those who believe it and join it, find that God is not trying to restrict them but to release them. He has designed us to play a part in His story, but until our sin is removed and forgiven we are sin's slave, held back from operating according to that design.

Genuine freedom comes to those who want to be different. The way of life the Bible calls "**flesh**" is always a life of bondage. But a life of liberty is always a life of righteousness, not doing right all the time but trusting in the One who does right all the time. Instead of being in Adam and bound to His limitations, we are by faith in Christ and able to partake of His righteousness. We now belong to the community of those who also trust Him for righteousness and life. As long as we are motivated by trying to belong, and trying to get in, our behavior will never permanently change. But God invites us to belong by faith and to behave like the people we are.

HE HAS DESIGNED US TO PLAY A PART IN HIS STORY, BUT UNTIL OUR SIN IS REMOVED AND FORGIVEN WE ARE SIN'S SLAVE, HELD BACK FROM OPERATING ACCORDING TO THAT DESIGN.

We are also freed from purposelessness and boredom so that we do not need television, video games, and hobbies to fill up empty hours. We do not have to spend our lives watching other people do exciting things. Some people reach their later years and worry about being bored. They see their kids and grandkids, some play golf and watch movies, then get together with friends their age and talk about their surgeries. But being an actor in God's script is far better and it takes a lifetime to do it right. It is a life that may well create conflict or elicit insults. The gospel of Jesus always requires a response, either for or against, but never apathy. The right response is to accept God's invitation to become a part of His story, step into the present future and live out the fulfillment available in Jesus Christ. ■

All Scriptures are King James Version unless otherwise indicated.

by Wade E. Taylor

> **"Now as he walked by the sea of Galilee, he saw Simon and Andrew his brother casting a net into the sea: for they were fishers.**
>
> **And Jesus said unto them, Come ye after me, and I will make you to become fishers of men.**
>
> **And straightway they forsook their nets, and followed him" (Mark 1:16-18).**

The **"net"** is whatever we may use to draw to ourselves the fulfillment and satisfaction we seek.

Simon and Andrew were casting their nets to catch fish. When Jesus came, He used words that they could easily understand. He told them that if they would follow Him, He would make them **"fishers of men."**

Notice that Jesus did not say He would show them "how" to fish for men. Rather, He said that He would make them to **"become"** fishers. The emphasis was not on methodology, but rather on the Lord's desire to draw them to Himself, in order to change them.

We Must First "Have" in Order to "Give"

> **"And hast made us unto our God kings and priests; and we shall reign on the earth" (Revelation 5:10).**

The emphasis is on our being made ready to reign, not on the fact of reigning. Many place great emphasis on the program (net) that is used to accomplish a certain purpose, rather than seeking to develop the ability to rightly use the program. We cannot give what we do not have. Therefore, it is very important that we spend quality time in the presence of the Lord and develop a strong spiritual relationship with Him. Only then will we "have" in order to "give."

Becoming a "Witness"

> **"But ye shall receive power, after that the Holy Ghost is come upon you: and ye shall be witnesses unto me both in Jerusalem, and in all Judea, and in Samaria, and unto the uttermost part of the earth" (Acts 1:8).**

The word **"witnesses"** can be translated "sample." For example, I once asked the salesperson in a large carpet store if I could have a sample of a huge roll of fifteen-foot wide carpet. He cut out a piece and handed it to me.

Because he had cut a piece from the end of this carpet, the entire fifteen-foot area was lost. But I had asked for a sample, so he gave me a piece of the real thing, which was costly to him, rather than something that was similar.

Here, the Lord is placing the emphasis on our becoming a "sample" of Himself, developed through an ongoing personal relationship with Him. Often, the emphasis has tended toward two extremes, either "asceticism" or "activity."

In the early church, there were those who became known as "Desert Fathers." They considered the world to be so wicked that they went out into the desert and lived in caves so they could be separated, and as a result become "spiritual."

But Jesus said that we were not to hide our light under a bushel. We are to be in the world, but the world is not to be in us. Rather, our light is to shine before men. We are to become a "witness" of the life and ministry of Jesus by becoming a "sample" of Him, a piece of the real thing in a place of need.

WE ARE TO BE IN THE WORLD, BUT THE WORLD IS NOT TO BE IN US.

The Process of Becoming

The president of a Bible school had a reputation for being a very spiritual man. A student decided he would find out if this was true. He went to the president's office and began fumbling with a bottle of ink and then "accidentally" spilled some on the president's suit.

The president began to get agitated, as he had cautioned him to be careful with the ink. But he gained his composure, smiled, and said it was all right. Soon the ink disappeared, since it was made to do this and was harmless. The student then told him he was just checking to see if he was as spiritual as others had said, and left satisfied.

In our becoming a sample or a "demonstration," of the presence and power of the Lord, there will be many occasions in which it will be easy to be otherwise. Jesus said, **"I will make you**

to become." This is a processing of the Lord to prepare us to rightly respond in these situations. Thus, those who are to rule are presently being prepared for this purpose.

As we allow the cross to become effective in our lives, and we die to our feelings and reactions, allowing Jesus be seen through our lives, we will indeed begin to catch "fish."

"Being" Rather Than "Doing"

The other extreme is "doing." To many, the baptism in the Holy Spirit is considered to be "power for service." These place the emphasis on going out to do witnessing, which may result in running without the message.

Peter probably heard the word "fishing" and did not realize all that he was about to experience in being "processed" to become the witness that the Lord intended him to be.

When Peter told the Lord he would die for Him, Jesus responded that instead he would deny Him. Peter reacted, but soon learned that we tend to promise the Lord many things, which we are incapable of doing. But the Lord has provided a way for us to go beyond these cycles of failure. He says: **"Follow Me and I will make you to become."**

As we allow the Lord to do a deep work within our lives in cleansing and purifying our motives, we are changed as the "power" renovates and recreates our lives to reflect His life. Only then there will be nothing in us to react.

Letting His Presence and Blessings Become Evident

It has been said that no one can "get our goat" unless we have one. As a child, I remember how kids would tease and pick on certain other children. Later I came to understand that these were being picked on because they reacted. The greater the reaction, the more they were picked on, as other kids enjoyed the reaction.

We tend to promise the Lord many things, which we are incapable of doing.

The enemy of our spiritual life also does this. When we react to dealings or problems and put on a show, the enemy gathers to enjoy our reaction. But if we have our feet on the Rock, and understand that we are being processed, the enemy will be defeated and will leave, since there will be no reaction to enjoy. Jesus said, **"...for the ruler of the world is coming, and he has nothing in Me" (John 14:30 NAS).**

In effect, Acts 1:8 reads, "You will receive power...to become." The desire of the Lord is to so change us that only His life will be seen. Therefore, all we need to do is to say, "Lord, I am available and willing to receive."

Only then will we become the "message" that people will respond to; our lives will be so changed by the power of God, that His presence and blessings are evident. ■

THY FACE OH LORD I WILL SEEK

by Francis Frangipane

There are some things in life that can not be attained cheaply or superficially. Scores of Scriptures call us to something much more consuming and fulfilling than just having a religion about Jesus Christ. Yet, the challenge is to focus and centralize our efforts to appropriate what Jesus came to give.

> **"For the coming of the Son of Man will be just like the days of Noah.**
>
> **"For as in those days which were before the flood they were eating and drinking, they were marrying and giving in marriage, until the day that Noah entered the ark,**
>
> **and they did not understand until the flood came and took them all away; so shall the coming of the Son of Man be" (Matthew 24:37-39).**

The biggest battle many fight is to stay focused on God long enough to learn how to abide in His presence. Before we can redeem the world, we must redeem our time. We would think that with all the time saving conveniences we have in life that this would be easy, but it is not.

The real test at the end of the age is: Can we live in a place of focused renewal? Those whom I have known who have fallen into sin never were taken in suddenly by the enemy. Their failure was always precipitated by an earlier erosion of their focus; their time with God was incrementally replaced with non-spiritual things. Left without the help of God, Satan's temptation came to a heart vulnerable and without strength to resist.

"But be sure of this, that if the head of the house had known at what time of the night the thief was coming, he would have been on the alert and would not have allowed his house to be broken into" (Matthew 24:43).

Speaking of the devil, Jesus warned that the **"thief comes only to steal, and kill and destroy" (John 10:10).** Beloved, the first thing the devil steals is time. Once we surrender our devotional time with God to non-spiritual things—once this world becomes more important to us than the next, the enemy has easy access to **"kill and destroy"** our virtue and spiritual strength.

And, if there is a decision to be made about doing His will, I must always choose Him above everyone else's interests, even my own.

Again, Jesus taught a parable about a certain man who was having a banquet and **"...he sent his slave to say to those who had been invited, 'Come; for everything is ready now.' But they all alike began to make excuses" (Luke 14:17-18).**

When the Lord calls us to Himself, do we make excuses? *I'm tired, hungry, or busy.* Jesus tells us that the reasons for avoiding Him will seem legitimate: **"...I have bought a piece of land and I need to go out and look at it; please consider me excused... I have bought five yoke of oxen, and I am going to try them out; please consider me excused...I have married a wife, and for that reason I cannot come" (Luke 14:18-20).**

I know it seems radical, but Jesus' final point is so contrary to the image we have of Him that His next admonition seems almost non-Christian. Let me also remind you that He was not only talking to His apostles or other "higher ups" in His staff; He turned and spoke to the **"great multitudes** [which] **were going along with Him" (Luke 14:25).**

"If anyone comes to Me, and does not hate his own father and mother and wife and children and brothers and sisters, yes, and even his own life, he cannot be My disciple.

"Whoever does not carry his own cross and come after Me cannot be My disciple" (Luke 14:26-27).

Here is how His Words strike my heart. To me, He is saying that I must not let any relationship challenge His love and call upon my life. And, if there is a decision to be made about doing His will, I must always choose Him above everyone else's interests, even my own. By comparison, every other relationship I have could appear like hate when measured by my love and obedience to Jesus.

Of course, loving Jesus brings the very best of heaven into all my other relationships; I possess something of Christ's life that brings *greater* love back to my family and friends, and even my own soul. But above all, the choice must be made for Christ.

You say, "This doesn't sound like the Jesus I know; He loves everyone." Yes, but He also knows the battle for our souls will be fierce and that to be successful in our spiritual journey, He must be first.

A Time to Seek God

There are many seasons in life. Ecclesiastes tells us there **"is a time for every purpose under heaven" (Ecclesiastes 3:1 NKJV).** Beloved, I believe it is time to draw near to God, to prepare our hearts for His presence. There simply is no substitute for the presence of God.

David was a king. His life was filled with many responsibilities and he was clearly very passionate about many things. Yet he wrote, **"When Thou didst say, 'Seek My face,' my heart said to Thee, 'Thy face, O LORD, I shall seek'" (Psalm 27:8).**

If the Holy Spirit were to whisper to your heart that He wants more of your time, when the Lord says, **"Seek My face,"** what do you say? Oh beloved, here is the true battle for your soul. Your victory is not in getting more counseling, but in your answer to the Lord's call.

The result of seeking God is that He guides us into an absolutely fearless life (see Psalm 27:1-4). David says, **"For in the day of trouble He will conceal me in His tabernacle; in the secret place of His tent He will hide me; He will lift me up on a rock" (Psalm 27:5).**

Today, with so many distractions, what place does the Lord have in your life? If He called you to deepen your walk, to seek His face, how would you respond? When He says, **"Seek My face,"** what does your heart say to Him? ■

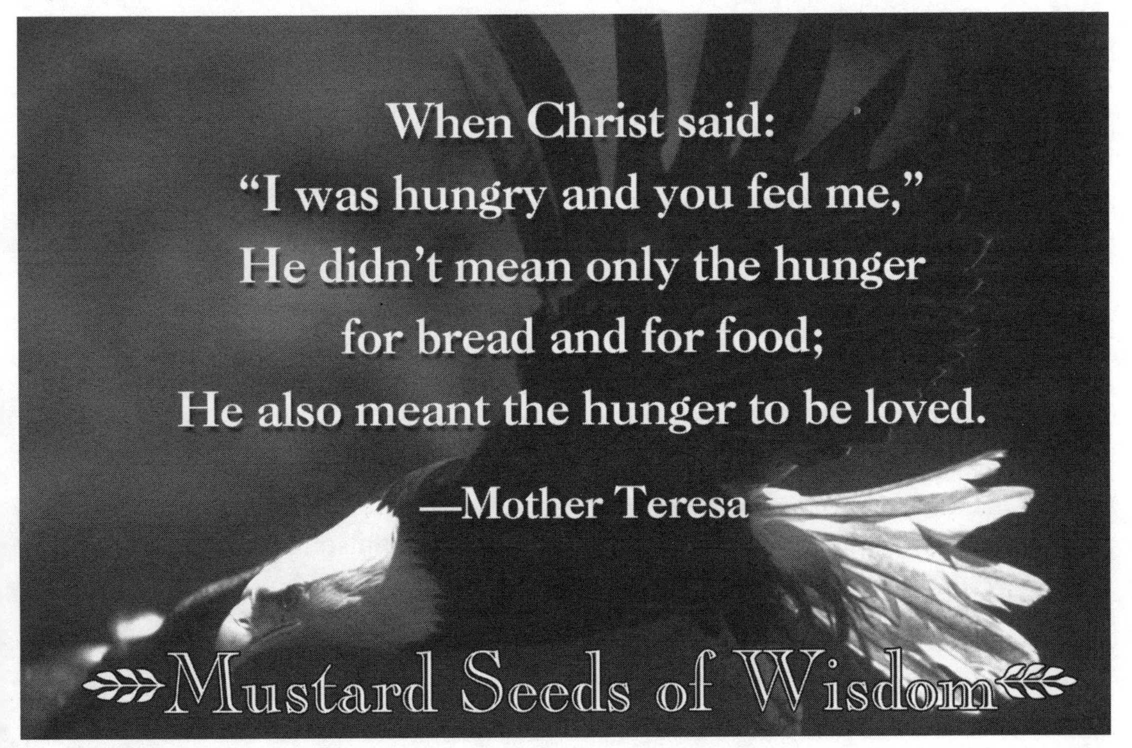

DISCERNING THE TIMES

by Rick Joyner

During the last year I have felt increasingly compelled to discern the times. As you may have heard me often confess, knowing God's timing, even concerning prophecies He has given through me, has been one of my great weaknesses. As I look at the body of Christ in general, I do not think that I am alone. In fact, I only know a couple of prophetic people who seem to accurately understand the timing of their own prophecies, but most of the time they too confess that they do not know the timing of their words. Even though I think this is one of our great weaknesses, the Lord is going to change this soon—He is going to begin to give us increasing understanding of timing.

It seems that the common approach to a problem such as this is to study it—acquire the knowledge of those in Scripture and history that seemed to have the valuable gift of understanding the times. However, the Scriptures teach that the real foundation for this knowledge is not mere knowledge as much as it is character. We will say more about this in a moment, but in our approach to any such issue we must always keep in mind that the answers we are seeking are always found in the Lord Himself, and being conformed to His image. The Lord Jesus Himself is the answer to every human problem.

THE BIBLICAL STANDARD

If we look at the biblical standard of knowing the times for prophecies given, it seems that only a small percentage of the prophecies given had a time attached to them. Basic to understanding prophecy is the truth of I Corinthians 13:9: **"For we know in part, and we prophesy in part..."** In spite of the spectacular prophetic gifts that are now being given to many, and the stunning supernatural knowledge demonstrated at times, the Lord never intended for prophecy to be an exact science. By this I am not speaking about accuracy, but prophecy is seldom intended to be comprehensive—giving us all of the details. Then we would not need to continue to seek Him, or to follow Him day by day with sensitivity, faith, and obedience.

It is a biblical truth that only those who are committed to following Him daily with sensitivity, faith, and obedience will hear His Words and interpret them accurately, as the Lord Himself asserted in John 7:17-18:

> **If any man is willing to do His will, he shall know of the teaching, whether it is of God, or whether I speak from Myself.**
>
> **He who speaks from himself seeks his own glory; but He who is seeking the glory of the One who sent Him, He is true, and there is no unrighteousness in Him.**

Here we see that to discern even the Lord Jesus' teachings, one had to be willing to do the will of God. This is the primary issue. As we seek the truth, are we willing to obey it? I have found that most people who claim to be seeking the truth in a matter are in reality actually seeking to confirm what they already believe, or what they want to believe. This is a foundation for deception and has been true in science which claims so much objectivity, even though it has generally been less objective than any other discipline. It is also true in theology and the pursuit of biblical knowledge, which can be very different from biblical truth.

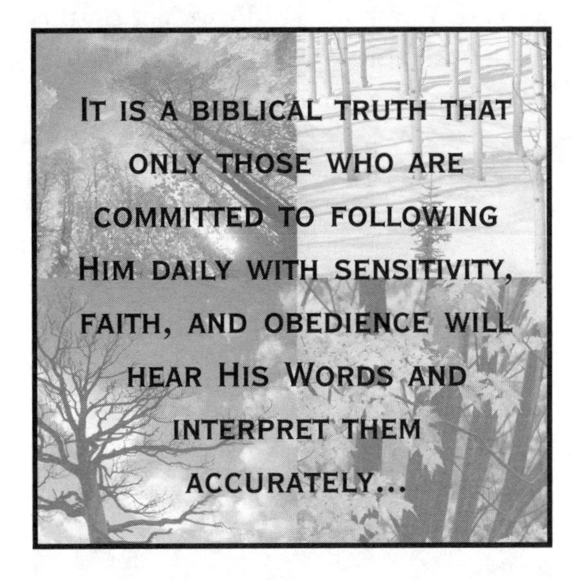

In the verses quoted above, Jesus also said that those who were speaking from themselves instead of from God could be discerned by their desire to seek their own glory, or as it could have been literally translated, their own "recognition." Therefore, the motives of the one teaching or prophesying are crucial. Nothing will more quickly pervert a prophetic ministry than the desire to be known as a prophet. Nothing will pervert a teaching ministry more quickly than wanting our teachings to be popular, or our books to be purchased, etc.

This does not mean that one has to be perfect to prophesy. If this were true the Lord Jesus would have been the only One capable of prophesying throughout history. However, self-seeking and self-promotion are the most destructive forces of perversion in any ministry. We may have many other flaws, but these two specifically cannot be tolerated or our ministry will be perverted. The more devoted we are to seeing the Lord glorified, and the less we care about any credit we get on this earth, the more true we will be, and the more truth we can be trusted with.

TO REPRESENT OR SPEAK FOR GOD, ONE HAS TO BE FREE FROM THE FEAR OF MAN AND THE DESIRE FOR THE PRAISES OF MAN, AND SEEK THEIR COMFORT AND ACCEPTANCE FROM GOD.

I do believe that I have this from the Lord—the truth about the end times will not be popular with the church. So if popularity is our motive, we will not teach the truth on this subject, as well as other important biblical truths that are crucial for walking in truth and discerning truth. As we see in II Thessalonians 2:10, it is not just those who receive truth who are not deceived, but those who receive a **"love of the truth."** There can be a big difference between the two. The latter will embrace the truth regardless of how uncomfortable it makes them or how unpopular it is.

It is for this reason that most true prophets are not received or recognized in their own time, and are continually rejected, scorned, and persecuted. Very few prophets have been what we would consider even socially acceptable in most circles. For that matter, very few apostles have been either. To represent or speak for God, one has to be free from the fear of man and the desire for the praises of man, and seek their comfort and acceptance from God.

The less you are affected by the opinions of people, the less comfortable people will be with you. Therefore, the only ones who will tend to listen to you will be those who want God and His truth enough to put up with you. This is the reason why Jesus Himself even came in a form that no one would be attracted to. He did not want anyone drawn to His appearance or His social position, but only by the Spirit and a love for the truth. As the Lord Jesus Himself warned in Luke 6:26: **"Woe to you when all men speak well of you, for in the same way their fathers used to treat the false prophets."** How much are we motivated by a desire to be accepted and popular with men?

In Revelation 8:1 it says, **"And when He broke the seventh seal, there was silence in heaven for about half an hour."** A popular interpretation of this is when everyone is burning their end time charts! I do believe that the most popular teachings on the end times are very far from the truth, and are in basic conflict with the Scriptures themselves, but the overwhelming majority of Christians seem to be completely unaware of these conflicts in doctrine. There is still a tendency to think that there is security in numbers, and if so many people believe them, they must be true. This concept itself, that truth is found in numbers, is in conflict with the entire weight of Scripture.

BEARERS OF THE TRUTH

In Matthew 11:25-26 we have another astonishing statement by the Lord concerning those who can discern truth: **"I praise Thee, O Father, Lord of heaven and earth, that Thou didst hide these things from the wise and intelligent and didst reveal them to babes. Yes, Father, for thus it was well-pleasing in Thy sight."** In the Greek, from which this is translated, it implies that the Lord was a little more than just thankful for this—He was ecstatic! This principle of the Father touched Him deeply. The things that touch Him need to be the things that touch us. The things that He esteems need to be the things that we esteem. So what is my point?

There are many doctrines concerning the last days from many established and popular sources, but they are not true. They will mislead multitudes for they do not love the truth more than they love appearances and the praises of men. At the same time, God is giving extraordinary revelation to children concerning the end times. Much of the greatest and most important revelation concerning those times, which we are going to need in the coming days, is going to come through children, which is what the Lord Himself was rejoicing about in the verses quoted in Matthew 11.

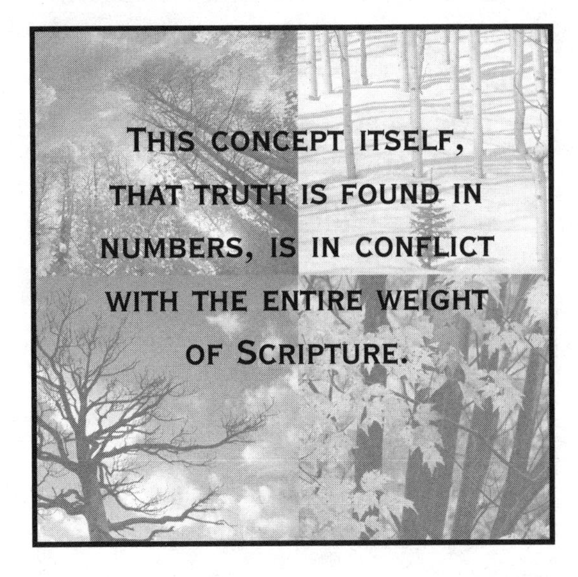

It is for this reason that we have been so committed to children's ministry and raising up children's prophetic teams. If you have attended any of our conferences, you have probably heard me say that we were really babysitting the adults so that the Lord could teach the children. This is not entirely accurate, as we care very much that everyone who comes receives all for which they came. But in truth we know that what is done in the children will bear the most long-term fruit, and so it is very crucial to us. One of our main goals for every child that attends our children's conferences is for each of them to know that they can hear from God, and leave knowing His voice better. We try to lay a foundation that, even if we never see them again, will be something they can grow on for their entire life.

We also try to continually remind ourselves that we must become like children to enter the kingdom of God. Our goal is more than just knowing what is coming—we want to be a part of it. We are going to need some of the same characteristics that children have if we are going to do this:

1) They tend to trust, not doubt.
2) They are teachable.
3) They are open to the Spirit.
4) They love freely.

WHO WARNED *THEM*?

When I teach these things or share them with other leaders I usually am asked if I am concerned with the way people will take this, even accusing us of letting children establish our doctrines and beliefs. I do expect to get such accusations, and would probably be even a little disappointed if we did not. People who tend to think in such ways are those we want to keep far from our ministry. These are the ones who are the kind of leaven that can ruin the whole lump.

I was once at a ranch spending a few days with several Christian leaders who all had or were growing in worldwide influence in the body of Christ. When everyone wanted to take a nap one afternoon, one of these men, who at the time was certainly one of the two or three most influential men in the church, wanted to stay and talk to me. His purpose was to convince me to change my writing and speaking style to reach theologians and conservative evangelicals. He felt that if I reached them, I would reach everyone else. I told him that I did not want to write for those people or for the professional Christians, but for those who had faith and a love for the truth, who were far more likely to be the common people.

My friend was strongly disagreeing with me when Paul Cain came stumbling out of his room with his eyes wide, saying he had just had a remarkable dream. In this dream Paul saw John the Baptist preaching. When the Pharisees and Sadducees came to him for baptism, John was angry, saying, **"who warned *you* to flee from the wrath to come?" (Matthew 3:7)**. I believe that John the Baptist felt this way because he knew these would one day do great damage to the church, and he was right.

All I said to my friend was, "That's what I meant to say!" As dramatically as I felt my position was confirmed in this, my friend remained unconvinced. In my opinion, his whole ministry began to slide at that point, and the great movement he had begun, started to lose its bearings. Soon the prophets he had recently publicly confessed to have "saved" his movement, started to get blamed for everything that went wrong, and far too soon he passed away.

I confess to likewise being more alarmed than pleased when some types of people are drawn to our ministry. I begin examining myself to see what I am doing wrong, wondering if we have started compromising in some way. I almost continually have people saying how sorry they are about all of the false things that are said about me, especially the things written on the Internet. They do not understand that this actually encourages me—I would be far more bothered if those same people were writing good things about me.

To be theologically correct is to be politically incorrect in much of the church. If you are concerned about being popular, you will never embrace the truth. This is what Paul was referring to in I Corinthians 3:18-21:

> **Let no man deceive himself. If any man among you thinks that he is wise in this age, let him become foolish that he may become wise.**
>
> **For the wisdom of this world is foolishness before God. For it is written, "He is the one who catches the wise in their craftiness";**
>
> **and again, "The Lord knows the reasonings of the wise, that they are useless."**
>
> **So then let no one boast in men.**

Those who receive human, worldly esteem and honor should set off alarms in us—not attract us to them as Paul also wrote in I Corinthians 1:26-29:

> **For consider your calling, brethren, that there were not many wise according to the flesh, not many mighty, not many noble;**
>
> **but God has chosen the foolish things of the world to shame the wise, and God has chosen the weak things of the world to shame the things which are strong,**
>
> **and the base things of the world and the despised, God has chosen, the things that are not, that He might nullify the things that are,**
>
> **that no man should boast before God.**

Here he does not say there are not *any* wise, mighty, noble, etc., but there are "**not *many*.**" We are coming to the end of this age, and it will be the time when the full result of the pride of man will be demonstrated for what it is. If we are going to remain true, we must learn to flee from many of the things that the world and the worldly church so esteems in its leaders.

ONE OF THE MOST ENCOURAGING THINGS FOR ME LATELY HAS BEEN TO SEE HOW THE PEOPLE WHO ATTEND OUR CONFERENCES RESPOND TO THE CHILDREN WHOM WE HAVE LET SPEAK IN OUR MAIN SERVICES.

THE FOUNDATIONS OF TRUTH

Faith and humility are the pillars of truth upon which all true wisdom and understanding are built. **"And without faith it is impossible to please Him, for he who comes to God must believe that He is, and that He is a rewarder of those who seek Him" (Hebrews 11:6).** Those who are more prone to doubt new things they hear rather than believe, will not come to the knowledge of the truth. This does not mean we should not have discernment and thoroughly check out the things that we hear in the Scriptures. However, it does mean that our basic tendency should be to believe, hope, and trust, rather than doubt. Skepticism and criticism have all of the appearances of wisdom, but it is a worldly wisdom that will inevitably end up in basic conflict with the Holy Spirit and the truth.

We read in James 4:6, **"God is opposed to the proud, but gives grace to the humble"** (see also I Peter 5:5). One of the basic characteristics of true humility is to be teachable. If we really want to know how humble we are or how teachable we really are, consider how we respond to someone we consider being less mature than we are.

One of the most encouraging things for me lately has been to see how the people who attend our conferences respond to the children whom we have let speak in our main services. We have had children as young as six years old speak to thousands. That they would have the courage to do this is amazing to many, but what they have to say is far more astonishing. We do not even help them prepare their messages either. We just tell them to speak what the Lord is saying to them.

Over and over we are told that the children, who speak at the conferences, as well as in our church services, are the highlights of those meetings. They often really do bring the most pure words from the Lord, and it comes with His anointing, which has at times left us all speechless. The truth, wisdom, faith, depth, and power, which come through these children, have brought deep conviction to thousands.

We had better learn to listen to our children. The children are for signs and wonders (see Isaiah 8:18), and **"from the mouth of infants and nursing babes Thou hast established strength..." (Psalm 8:2,** see also Matthew 21:16). If you really want your church to be prepared for the times to come, invest in your children's ministry. It is a great spiritual crime to have a children's ministry that only baby-sits so the parents can enjoy the "real service."

If we want the truth, we also need to listen to the humble even more in some ways than those who are of reputation. The Lord does raise up elders in the church whose words should carry weight. But if you only want a prophetic word from someone who is of great reputation, you will almost certainly miss the majority of what the Lord is trying to say to you. I know many who come to our conferences want a personal prophecy from Paul Cain or Bob Jones. But it is one of my great joys to see so many dignified leaders of great churches go in to receive ministry from our children's prophetic teams and come out not only in tears, but sometimes crawling on their knees. We have received letters stating that these encounters with the children were not only the highlight of the conference for them, but were actually highlights in their lives.

SAUL AND PAUL

Though what I have written above is sound, biblical truth, there will always be some "Sauls" who are converted and become "Pauls." By this I mean that there are some theologians and church leaders who are more professionals than true shepherds, who can be converted and can become some of the greatest teachers and leaders of all. We should not give up on any person as long as they are alive, but I certainly will not trust one of these until they have been converted.

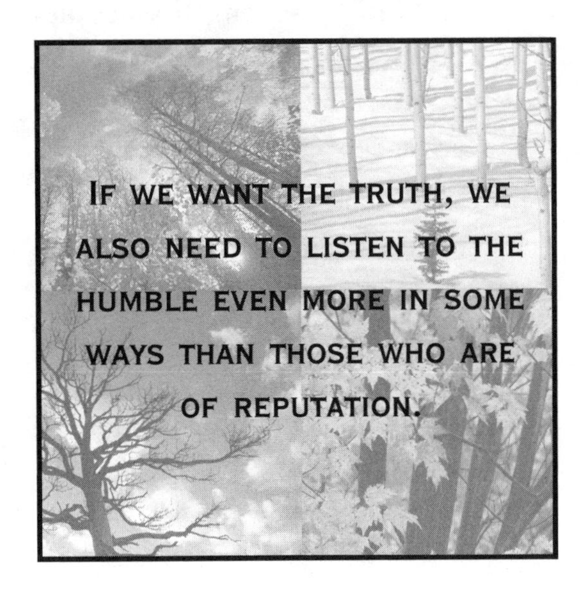

Like John the Baptist and the Lord Jesus Himself, if there is anyone that we should view with skepticism when they come to us, it is these "professional church leaders." There are many pastors and theologians who are in a profession, rather than a calling. We should be able to discern the difference, but few can because we are more devoted to what we perceive to be "excellence" and what attracts people, than we are able to recognize the anointing.

Even after his conversion, the church was right to be wary of Paul until he had proved himself over time. More damage has been done to the church by "professional" Christian leaders and theologians than all of the other attacks by the devil combined. The greatest deception and perversion of the church came when positions in the church gained political authority and wealth, and were then sought and attained by those who desired these things more than they wanted to serve the Lord by serving His people. True leaders, who walk the way of the cross, and who humble themselves doing their work as servants, are still very rare.

However, there is a new breed arising. There are already many children in our midst who have more authority in heaven than many of the most highly visible and popular leaders of our time. Those who are spiritually wise and discerning will know this change is upon us and will begin to discern the times. We are going to begin to receive clarity and accuracy in relation to the times, and the biblical prophecies concerning the end of this age, as we are told in I Thessalonians 5:1-6:

Now as to the times and the epochs, brethren, you have no need of anything to be written to you.

For you yourselves know full well that the day of the Lord will come just like a thief in the night.

While they are saying, "Peace and safety!" then destruction will come upon them suddenly like birth pangs upon a woman with child; and they shall not escape.

But you, brethren, are not in darkness, that the day should overtake you like a thief;

for you are all sons of light and sons of day. We are not of night nor of darkness;

so then let us not sleep as others do, but let us be alert and sober.

Just as the apostle is stating here, those who are of the light should not be overtaken by the day as by a thief. Things that are coming upon the world should not surprise us. The Lord is raising up a prophetic ministry, which will not be caught off guard by any major events, and they will see the moves of God coming with great accuracy. However, prophetic ministry is not going to come in a package like most of us want it to come in. Have faith, but stay humble and teachable, and you will be able to discern it and receive it. You may even be able to become a part of it. ■

THE LORD IS RAISING UP A PROPHETIC MINISTRY, WHICH WILL NOT BE CAUGHT OFF GUARD BY ANY MAJOR EVENTS, AND THEY WILL SEE THE MOVES OF GOD COMING WITH GREAT ACCURACY.

Victory Over Impatience

by Deborah Joyner Johnson

God is never in a hurry.

—Oswald Chambers

In a world that has every convenience at its fingertips, the word "patience" will have a negative connotation to most. Our world has become fast-paced with computer technology, video games, television, and movies, which have become so dramatic that "edge of the seat" experiences happen one after another. We have fast food restaurants with very little waiting and microwave dinners that may be heated and eaten in a matter of minutes. Flying across the country takes a matter of hours and within seconds we can be on the phone with someone in another country. These conveniences may be helpful, but they may also be detrimental if we expect everything to come to us this quickly.

If we are impatient we will have a tendency to be self-centered and lead stressful lives. Peace will not be a part of our lives because we are in too much of a hurry to embrace the rest and peace the Lord desires for us to have. There is a restlessness associated with impatient people and it will actually stop the flow of creativity. If we are impatient, work usually amounts to little or nothing because of the tendency to finish the project too quickly. Work that is hurried is only mediocre at best.

When we become impatient, frustration may cause us to take matters into our own hands. We may fulfill a fleshy desire, but such impatience will cause us to miss God's best. Remember the story of Ishmael. Because of impatience and unbelief, Sarah gave Hagar, her maid, to Abraham as a wife so she could have a child through her. Abraham displayed unbelief by not waiting to have a child through Sarah. As soon as the child was conceived, Sarah knew that her scheme had been wrong, but there was no turning back. Hagar's son was Ishmael, and from his lineage came the religion Islam, a distortion and great enemy of Israel and Christianity.

...there is a correlation between faith and patience—the more faith we have in our lives, the more patient we will be.

Patience, a Virtue

Patience must be a virtue within us if we are ever to accomplish anything of worth in this life. Most accomplishments do not come easily, so we must know from the beginning that it will take work, diligence, perseverance, and patience to accomplish goals.

What does it means to be patient? James 1:2-4 states:

> **My brethren, count it all joy when you fall into various trials,**
>
> **knowing that the testing of your faith produces patience.**
>
> **But let patience have its perfect work, that you may be perfect and complete, lacking nothing (NKJV).**

According to James, we should be happy when we encounter trials because **"the testing of your faith produces patience."** First, let us think about the word **"testing."** When I looked up this word in the *Webster's Dictionary*, I was astounded at one of the meanings—"an event, set of circumstances, etc. that proves or tries a person's qualities." Faith should actually be a quality in our character. When it is tested and proven, and we do indeed have faith, then patience will grow within us. So we can conclude from this Scripture that there is a correlation between faith and patience—the more faith we have in our lives, the more patient we will be.

According to Hebrews 6, it takes **"faith and patience" (Hebrews 6:12)** to inherit the promises. But to have both we must allow faith to produce patience within us. When we have faith, we do not need evidence to believe—we just know that whatever we believe will happen, no matter how long it takes. This indeed is patience. When we are patient, we do not complain but endure the waiting. Lamentations 3:25 states: **The LORD is good to those who wait for Him, to the person who seeks Him.**

The Israelites wandered in the desert for forty years because of their murmuring and complaining, which was basically rooted in impatience. Let us learn now to remove complaining from our lives. When we complain, we are decreasing the faith within us, which will in turn decrease our patience.

"**Let patience have its perfect work, that you may be perfect and complete, lacking nothing.**" This is an amazing thought. If we can allow patience to be worked into our lives, we can actually be "**perfect and complete, lacking nothing.**" You may ask how can we be perfect and complete just by being patient? The Lord knows how difficult it is to be patient and if we can be perfected in this one area, then most likely we will have the other fruits of the Spirit in our lives as well. The fruits of the Spirit are: "**love, joy, peace, patience, kindness, goodness, faithfulness, gentleness, self-control...**" **(Galatians 5:22-23).** As we follow the Lord more deeply, these character traits should become who we really are. Paul explains to us in I Corinthians 13:4 that "**Love is patient**" so, we can conclude, to be patient is to love. If we are kind, we are patient. If we have goodness, we are patient. If we have faithfulness, we are patient, and so on. Now, we can see that to be patient is to be "**perfect and complete, lacking in nothing.**"

If we apply this to accomplishing our purposes in life, we must be patient and persevere through whatever circumstances may occur until that which we are working toward is completed. It is our faith that will produce the patience to finish our purposes. To have vision is to actually see (through faith) the end result of our goal *before* it happens. Faith and patience are connected.

As we work toward accomplishing goals, do it as unto the Lord, so it will please Him. As we do our work unto the Lord, we will want to do our very best. Many times we need to sit quietly (with patience!) and wait before the Lord, and then He will give us instructions on our purposes. Quality time spent with the Lord is never wasted. His inspiration is freely given if we will seek Him. Not only will we receive from Him, but our relationships will grow with Him. And after all, our time spent with Him is by far the most important time we will ever spend in our lives. Fulfilling our purposes should be an outgrowth from the special time we spend with Him. We should all be accomplishing great things because we have His creativity flowing through us, but doing works will never be as important as being with the Lord. "**Whatever you do, do your work heartily, as for the Lord rather than for men; knowing that from the Lord you will receive the reward of the inheritance...**" **(Colossians 3:23-24).**

To have vision is to actually see (through faith) the end result of our goal *before* it happens.

With faith and patience, you can accomplish your purpose. Do not lose sight of the One who will instruct you with His patience. He is the guide to finishing that which He has called you to do. ■

Impacting Your Workplace Prophetically

by Dr. Bill Hamon

As representatives of Jesus Christ and His kingdom, it is vitally important that Christians in the marketplace be fully operational in hearing God's voice and doing His works. We need to change our thinking to realize that this is at least as important, if not more so, for marketplace saints than for saints called to minister inside the local church. This is because business people operate in realms that are largely still under the power of darkness. (The terms "marketplace" and "business" here are referring to the 98 percent of Christians who make their primary living outside the local church, including those in government, education, the arts, media, sports, students, homemakers, etc.)

Every successful business enterprise in the Bible achieved its success based upon hearing the directive voice of God and properly following those directives. Whether it was building a ship or the temple, leading in business, in government, or in ministry, the projects undertaken by God's people were successful if they heard and heeded the word of the Lord.

Noah was instructed by the Lord to go into a shipbuilding business. He built his ship (ark) according to the revelation knowledge from God. Following prophetic directives caused his ship to stay afloat during the greatest economic and natural disaster ever to hit planet earth. While every business and living thing on earth was "liquidated," his business maintained and progressed to function in the new world.

Isaac had financial success while everyone around him was in economic recession. He received a prophetic word from God to stay in his geographic area even though famine was in the region. The Bible says he sowed at God's directive and timing and reaped a hundred-fold in the same year. Then he became rich and kept increasing in wealth until he became exceedingly wealthy. He became so prosperous that all the surrounding businesses became envious of him (see Genesis 26:1-12). Many other biblical examples, such as Abraham, Joseph, David, and Daniel show people prospering and gaining great positions of influence by following prophetic directives from the Lord.

People Can Still Hear From God Today

Regarding his experience in the business world, Ed Silvoso writes:

> *I thoroughly enjoyed dealing, buying, selling, and hiring. The pressure was always on but each time it approached the boiling point, I reached for what I called the Jesus chair. This was a chair I had purposely placed in my office. When things became unmanageable, I would close the door, kneel by the chair and ask for divine guidance. Repeatedly God provided it. Sometimes He did it in a quiet way. At other times He gave me specific directions. More than once He performed business miracles in answer to those prayers. It was so reassuring to know that Jesus was there and that He had anointed me for the job I had!* [Ed Silvoso, *Anointed for Business* (Ventura, CA: Regal, 2002), p. 30.]

Dr. Sanford Kulkin, one of Christian International's Board of Governors, is a present-day example of a prophet in the marketplace. As a high-level business consultant, Sandy not only has God-given wisdom for consultation, but at times he also pulls upon the Holy Spirit's gifts of words of knowledge and words of wisdom in giving wise recommendations. God has blessed him mightily and has used him to help major corporations save millions of dollars and prosper abundantly. Even those who are not called as a prophet or apostle need to use the gifts of the Spirit in their daily business.

Many other biblical examples...show people prospering and gaining great positions of influence by following prophetic directives from the Lord.

Hearing God to Be a Witness

Scripture makes it clear that God will speak to people to help them succeed in their enterprises. But He will also speak through them to be a witness of Himself to others. When those of us who function as pulpit ministers encounter persons out in the marketplace and are asked what we do for a living, it is not too difficult to determine how they feel about spiritual matters based upon how they receive our response. Sometimes this leads to an opening to talk about the Lord. Many of our traveling ministers regularly have opportunities to lead people to the Lord or speak into their lives on airplanes.

The Holy Spirit knows exactly when hearts are open and when the best impact can be made.

For example, one time when my daughter-in-law, Jane Hamon, was traveling on an airplane, she sensed the Spirit telling her that the man sitting next to her was a divine appointment. Although she really wanted to keep to herself, she obeyed the Lord and struck up a conversation. When the man asked what she did for a living, she replied that she and her husband pastored a church, then he became angry and began speaking abusively about Christians. She silently prayed and the Holy Spirit showed her two specific areas where he had been deeply wounded in the past in regard to religion. She told him that she believed that God loves people and speaks to them today and asked for permission to share with him what she felt He had to say. The man gave permission and she shared what the Lord showed her. He was in complete shock and admitted the truth of it. She was then able to lead him to the Lord.

All saints can be activated to hear the Lord this clearly. But saints who primarily function in the marketplace will need to trust the Holy Spirit not only for openings to speak to others, but also for the divine revelation to steer conversations toward spiritual matters.

Need to Recognize Divine Timing

Those called to "minister" in ungodly environments, especially those in environments that are openly hostile to the gospel, need to be able to hear the Holy Spirit at least as much as pulpit ministers. If a pulpit minister fails to heed the leading of the Spirit, he or she may preach a message that lacks the anointing and power to impact the lives of those listening. If he is a traveling minister, he may not be invited back again. But public school teachers, university professors, police officers, or government employees could endanger their jobs as well as their influence if they speak out of turn. In some countries, saints' lives are at stake every time they speak about Jesus. The Holy Spirit knows exactly when hearts are open and when the best impact can be made.

Miracles and Deliverance in the Marketplace

This is not to say that accurately hearing the Holy Spirit will keep saints from persecution, because the Bible is clear that those who live a godly life in Christ Jesus will suffer persecution (see II Timothy 3:12). But if, like Paul and Silas, we are in the will of the Lord, heeding the Holy Spirit, and we find ourselves in a "prison," we can rejoice knowing that God will use it to bring a greater salvation (see Acts 16:19-34). Paul and Silas received a supernatural miracle (an earthquake) to release their chains and provide a witness to the jailer. We can expect to see this more and more frequently as apostles, prophets, and other five-fold ministers are fulfilling their roles of equipping God's saints to do the work of the ministry (see Ephesians 4:11-13). God can perform miracles just as easily in the marketplace as in the local church, at times even more so because there may be less unbelief (see Matthew 13:58).

Training for Reigning

Believers today who want to be used mightily by God cannot expect to without having the full arsenal of God at their disposal. We are beginning to see average saints become like the prophet Elijah who challenged the prophets of Baal and won, demonstrating the supremacy of God to all Israel (see I Kings 18:1-40). But without the gifts of the Spirit in operation, saints will not know when to speak up, when to stay quiet, when to move, or when to stay put. Nor will they have the power when they need to manifest it. Training in hearing the voice of God and ministering in the gifts of the Spirit is urgently needed. It is no longer an option but has become a vital necessity for believers who want to participate in what the Holy Spirit is doing in the church today.

Choose You This Day

As history progresses to the end of the age, a greater dichotomy is forming between those who are in Christ and those who are in the world. The world is getting more and more demon-possessed and oppressed, while the church is becoming more and more glorious in Jesus. Those who want to maintain peace with both sides will not be able to for long. We are either going to be aggressively advancing the kingdom of God using all the divine enablements Christ has provided, or we will find ourselves actively opposing the move of God through His church. If your primary calling is outside the walls of the local church, you can be equipped to operate in the power of God and revolutionize your environment. Saints who prepare themselves to become full "believers" (see Mark 16:17-18), and who die to self to live for Christ and His kingdom, will be mightily used by God in the days just ahead. The time to prepare is now.

Believers today who want to be used mightily by God cannot expect to without having the full arsenal of God at their disposal.

*This article was excerpted from Dr. Hamon's book, **The Day of the Saints**, available from Christian International. Please call 800-388-5308 or see www.christianinternational.org.* ■

The Divine Nature

by Mike Roberts

"For what will a man be profited, if he gains the whole world, and forfeits his soul? Or what will a man give in exchange for his soul?" (Matthew 16:26)

This verse is familiar to most Christians, but in many cases, its meaning is probably not fully understood. Many people read this verse and interpret it to mean that it would not truly benefit a person if he acquires every possible treasure in this life, but then goes to hell when he dies. This is certainly an applicable interpretation, but Jesus was actually referring to more than this when He spoke those words.

A Lifelong Conflict

The Lord intends for a man's soul (mind, will, and emotions) and his spirit to exist in harmony, with his spirit being the dominant component in his personality. However, in most cases, the soul occupies the dominant position. This is not the way it was in the beginning. Derek Prince once said, *"The spirit of man comes directly from God and relates directly to God. In the original pattern of creation, there was a descending relationship. God moved upon man's spirit; his spirit moved upon his soul; and his soul directed his body."*[1] In most cases today, our souls are in conflict with our spirits, and all too often, our souls end up in charge. Most of us make our decisions based on what our natural man thinks, desires, and feels, instead of what God is saying to our spirits. This is a result of the fall of man in the garden (see Genesis 3:1-11).

Before Adam and Eve partook of the fruit from the tree of the knowledge of good and evil, they walked with God without anything hindering their relationship with Him. Once they had partaken of the forbidden fruit, they realized they were naked and they became ashamed. Genesis 3:7 says:

> **Then the eyes of both of them were opened, and they *knew* that they were naked; and they sewed fig leaves together and made themselves loin covering.**

For the first time in the life of Adam and Eve, a decision was made based on natural knowledge and not the Word of God. This does not mean that they were separated from the Lord for eternity. But to a degree, their souls became influenced and tarnished by the enemy. Suddenly, their minds, wills, and emotions were influenced partly by the enemy, and to that degree, the Lord lost His influence over their souls. Consequently, their souls, not their spirits, became the dominant components of their personalities. This resulted in their own ideas, knowledge, desires, and feelings coming between their spirits and the voice of the Lord. This is the same for many of us today. Therefore, we tend to be influenced more by our fallen nature than we are by the Holy Spirit.

The enemy knows that if he can cause our souls to preside over our spirits, he can interfere with our accomplishing the will of God. I John 2:15-17 says:

> **Do not love the world, nor the things in the world. If anyone loves the world, the love of the Father is not in him.**
>
> **For all that is in the world, the lust of the flesh and the lust of the eyes and the boastful pride of life, is not from the Father, but is from the world.**
>
> **And the world is passing away, and also its lusts; but the one who does the will of God abides forever.**

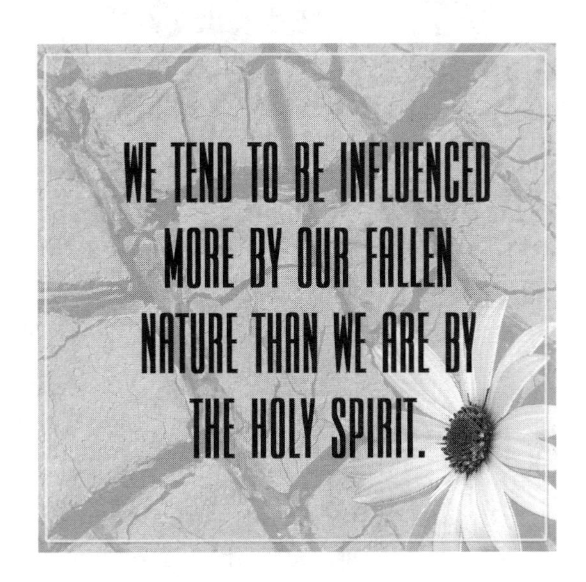

These verses list three things the enemy uses to distract us from the will of God: **"the lust of the flesh and the lust of the eyes, and the boastful pride of life."** In one way or another, every distraction from the enemy will fall into one of these three categories.

THE LUST OF THE FLESH

Lust is basically a desire to fulfill needs by inappropriate means. Many of the things we lust after are things God intends to give us, but lust will cause us to seek inappropriate means to attain them. The lust of the flesh is generally associated with sex, but although sexual lust is common, it can also involve more subtle desires. Some people lust after emotional fulfillment, or seek to inappropriately use another person to meet a sensual desire.

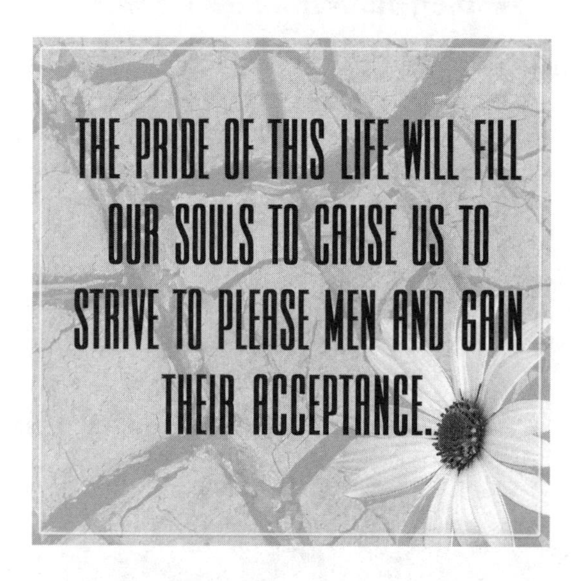

THE LUST OF THE EYES

The lust of the eyes is very similar to the lust of the flesh, but rather than lusting for sensual fulfillment, it is lusting after, or coveting, material possessions. In and of itself, there is nothing wrong with desiring material possessions, and many of the things we desire are things the Lord wants to give us. However, our desires become coveting when they dominate our thoughts and wishes. Coveting can cause us to seek to attain these by our natural strength outside of God's timing. A covetous person's soul will be consumed with a desire for material satisfaction more than a desire to do the will of God.

THE BOASTFUL PRIDE OF LIFE

The third form of lust that can be a distraction to our souls is the boastful pride of life. This is closely related with the lust of the eyes, but it entails much more. Pride of this type causes us to be more concerned with our earthly position than our position in eternity. Subtle pride will then begin to creep into a person's life during childhood and will linger as long as it is allowed. A child will bend to peer pressure to avoid losing his position of acceptance with friends. An adult will work endlessly for that "one more thing," not so he can have it, but so he can attain the position he believes it will bring. The pride of this life will fill our souls, causing us to strive to please men and gain their acceptance. This is an enemy to the will of God, as the apostle Paul explained:

> **For am I now seeking the favor men, or of God? Or am I striving to please men? If I were still trying to please men, I would not be a bond-servant of Christ (Galatians 1:10).**

THE WILL OF GOD

As we have seen, the things of the world are distractions to us as we seek to accomplish the will of God. They are ruthless, and their goal is to overtake our thoughts, desires, and feelings. If they succeed, all that we do will be temporary and ultimately fruitless, and we will be in bondage to our fallen nature. However, as we have also seen, we are called to do the will of God and to bear fruit that lasts for eternity. To accomplish this, our souls must be free of the entanglements of the world. Thankfully, the Lord has not left us to accomplish this alone. In our own strength we would surely fail, but He has made *His* divine nature available to us. II Peter 1:3-4 says:

> **seeing that His divine power has granted to us everything pertaining to life and godliness, through the true knowledge of Him who called us by His own glory and excellence.**
>
> **For by these He has granted to us His precious and magnificent promises, in order that by them you might become partakers of the divine nature, having escaped the corruption that is in the world by lust.**

These verses explain that lust has brought corruption to the world, but that we are able to live above this. His "**divine power**" has been made available to us all so we may live our lives in a way that is pleasing to the Lord. He has also said it is possible for us to "**become partakers of the divine nature.**" Our earthly nature gravitates toward the things of the world, but His divine nature pursues the things that are righteous and eternal. Becoming "**partakers of the divine nature**" is our remedy to the corruption that comes from lust. Let us briefly examine how we come to partake of the Lord's "**divine nature.**"

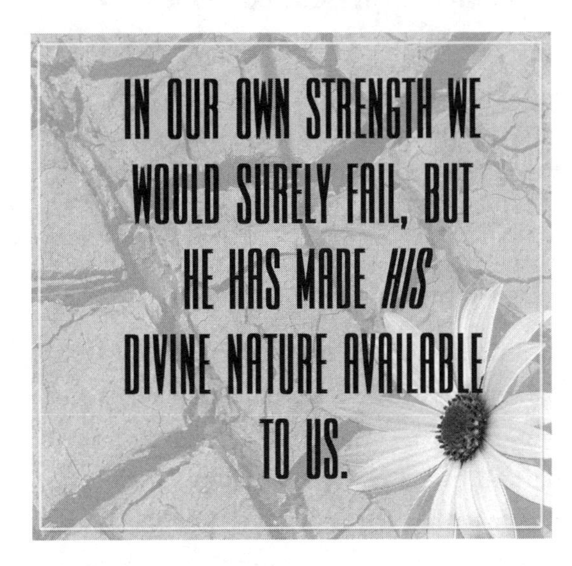

THE DIVINE NATURE

In this life we will become like whatever or whomever we behold. If we are beholding the things of the world, then we will begin to take on their likeness. But if we are beholding the Lord, we will begin to take on His likeness. II Corinthians 3:18 says:

> **But we all, with unveiled face beholding as in a mirror the glory of the Lord, are being transformed into the same image from glory to glory, just as from the Lord, the Spirit.**

We are changed into the image of the Lord and begin to partake of His nature as we walk with Him and behold Him. The more we partake of His nature, the less we will partake of our fallen nature, and the less we will become entangled with the things of the world.

> **Now may the God of peace Himself sanctify you entirely; and may your spirit and soul and body be preserved complete, without blame at the coming of our Lord Jesus Christ.**
>
> **Faithful is He who calls you, and He also will bring it to pass (I Thessalonians 5:23-24).**

CONCLUSION

These verses speak of the Lord sanctifying our entire being. To be sanctified means to be "set apart." As the Lord sanctifies us, He sets us apart for Himself that we may be untarnished by the things of the world. Let us, therefore, purpose to seek the Lord with all of our being—spirit, soul, and body. Let us guard our souls against diversions by the things of the world, and allow ourselves to be completely set apart for the Lord. As He sanctifies us, and as we behold Him, our spirits will once again claim its place of fellowship with the Lord. As this begins to happen, we will begin to walk in His divine nature, and our lives will be forever changed. We will no longer be subject to our fallen nature, but a proper relationship will develop between our spirits and our souls. Our thoughts will be pure and righteous, and our desires will be holy. Our feelings and emotions will be set apart unto the Lord, and we will live a life of victory and ever-increasing intimacy with the Lord. ■

[1]*Derek Prince Teaching Letter #11, "Spiritual or Soulish," www.derekprince.com*

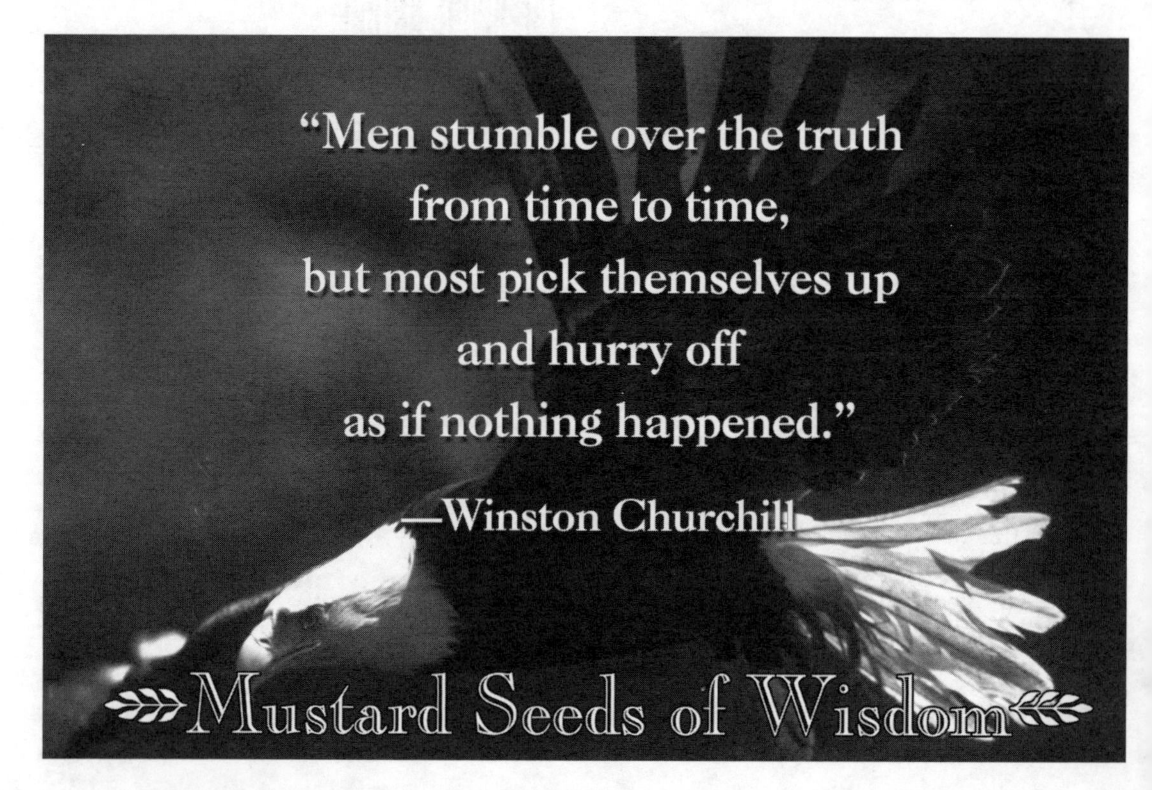

by Rick Joyner

A comprehensive study of the prophecies related to the end of this age would take many volumes. Therefore, what we are going to be covering in this study are the most important keys to understanding the coming times.

Just as a compass has four "cardinal points" from which all other directions are established (North, South, East and West), there are likewise four such cardinal points to understanding biblical prophecy. When we understand these, we can more accurately understand and navigate through the times. These four points to understanding biblical prophecy are:

1) **Our main goal should be to understand what God is doing, not what the devil is doing.**
2) **The tragedies and destruction that come upon the world are the result of man trying to live without God, and in rebellion to Him.**
3) **True discernment is based on love, not hatred or fear.**
4) **Our reason for being here in these times is to fulfill the Great Commission.**

Now we will briefly look at each of these cardinal points and see how they are related, and how they can give us direction for understanding and navigating through the times ahead.

CARDINAL POINT #1—Our main goal should be to understand what God is doing, not what the devil is doing.

We must keep our attention and focus on what Christ is going to do, not what the antichrist is going to do. This is our spiritual magnetic north from which all of the other points are determined in relation to biblical prophecy.

There are some things that we need to understand about the antichrist, and we do not want to be ignorant of the devil's schemes, just as the Scriptures teach us. However, if we become overly focused on the antichrist, and his purposes, they will divert us from a true understanding of the times. What the antichrist is doing is the sideshow, not the main event. If we spend too much time in the sideshow we are certain to miss the main events.

Those who become overly focused on the devil or the antichrist, inevitably start taking on his nature and become accusers of the brethren.

What the Lord is doing to prepare for His coming kingdom is the main event, which is what we want to see and be a part of. It will only be in the light of this that we will be able to clearly see what the devil or the antichrist is doing, or has done. Everything that the devil is doing is an attempt to counter the purposes of God.

We also want to keep in mind the principle of II Corinthians 3:18: **"But we all, with unveiled face beholding as in a mirror the glory of the Lord, are being transformed into the same image from glory to glory, just as from the Lord, the Spirit."** To simplify the principle stated here, we are going to become like that which we are beholding. Our goal is to become Christlike, which we do by beholding Him. Those who become overly focused on the devil or the antichrist, inevitably start taking on his nature and become accusers of the brethren.

Now the key word here is not to be "overly focused" on the devil and his purposes. Again, there are some things that we do need to understand or they would not be in the Scriptures. However, a third of the angels, or messengers, fell, which means that two-thirds did not fall. That means that the good angels outnumber the bad by two to one (not to mention the fact that God by Himself outnumbers them all!). My point is that in my studies of the end times, I try to devote at least twice as much attention to what God is doing as I do to what the devil is doing.

One main point that we need to keep in mind is: Where are we going? To navigate implies that we are trying to get somewhere. The answer to that question is—*the kingdom.* We need to keep in mind that this is not just the end of this age, but the beginning of the age to come in which our King is going to rule over the earth. He is coming to set up His kingdom, and we are His agents to prepare the way for it. Our purpose is to make His way straight, to proclaim the gospel of the kingdom throughout the world in preparation for His coming.

CARDINAL POINT #2—The tragedies and destruction that come upon the world are the result of man trying to live without God, and in rebellion to Him.

If we are going to understand the times, we must see beyond just what is happening and start to understand why it is happening. We must settle in our hearts that God is the answer to every human problem. The six thousand years of man's history will be an eternal witness of the folly of trying to live without God. Therefore, the first and most basic evidence that redemption has worked in our lives is that we start doing all that we do with Him, seeking in all things to abide in Him, and do His will.

As the Lord Himself said in John 7:17, **"If any man is willing to do His will, he shall know of the teaching, whether it is of God, or whether I speak from Myself."** Fundamental to knowing the truth is the determination to obey God. This again points us to the kingdom of God, which is composed of all who live in obedience to the King, which we are called to live in and represent to this world.

In contrast to this, we see in the Scriptures the great evil that brings so much destruction upon the world in the last days is *lawlessness.* It is noteworthy that many try to combat this increasing lawlessness with legalism, which is just another form of trying to do it without God. God's counter to lawlessness is not legalism, but is in fact the greatest freedom that we could ever know—the simplicity of devotion to Christ and following Him.

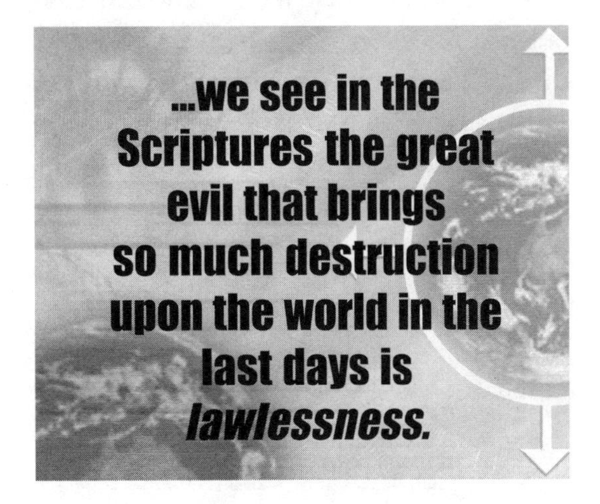

The One who made us knows better than we do what we were created for. A trail may think it is more "free" if it can leave its tracks to go wherever it wants, but it will quickly become mired and immobile. We, too, will quickly become mired in the greatest bondage of all when we depart from the tracks that God has established for our lives. The very things that may seem to hinder our freedom are what set us free to be what we were created to be.

If we follow Him, He will always lead us into triumph over the ways of this world, because a single life built on the Rock is stronger than all of the systems of this world. Therefore, the greatest freedom that we can ever experience on this earth is to be the King's slave. It is on the basis of this ultimate freedom that we can alone understand our times, and the prophecies of Scripture.

CARDINAL POINT #3—True discernment is based on love, not hatred or fear.

As Paul the apostle wrote in Philippians 1:9, **"And this I pray, that your love may abound still more and more in real knowledge and all discernment."** Anything but love will distort our discernment and our knowledge. This is one reason why we must even love our enemies. We will never be able to understand them or defeat them if we are controlled by fear or hatred of them.

Those who pierced Him will mourn, as will all who did not serve Him, but He is not coming back to gloat over His enemies.

We must also keep in mind that our victory over our enemies in the faith is to see them converted to Christ, which will end up being their greatest victory too. Love is our most powerful weapon, and true love is an irresistible force that will ultimately prevail.

There is a terrible mentality with some Christians that the Lord is returning to get even with all who rejected Him. He is not coming back to get even with anyone. He did not go to the cross in order to be able to destroy, but to save. He is coming back to restore all things that we lost by the Fall. He is going to restore the earth, and He is going to restore mankind to the state and purpose for which he was created. Redemption and restoration are the heart of God, not retaliation. Those who pierced Him will mourn, as will all who did not serve Him, but He is not coming back to gloat over His enemies. Let us banish that mentality far from us. It is contrary to Scripture and an affront to His character. It will also lead to our deception if we hold on to it. In all things let us remember I Timothy 1:5: **"...the goal of our instruction is love from a pure heart and a good conscience and a sincere faith."**

CARDINAL POINT #4—Our reason for being here in these times is to fulfill the Great Commission.

This is the purpose for which every Christian is now on the earth, as we read in Matthew 28:18-20:

> **And Jesus came up and spoke to them, saying, "All authority has been given to Me in heaven and on earth.**
>
> **"Go therefore and make disciples of all the nations, baptizing them in the name of the Father and the Son and the Holy Spirit,**
>
> **teaching them to observe all that I commanded you; and lo, I am with you always, even to the end of the age."**

Now let us briefly look at the main points of this commission:

1) All authority has been given to Jesus in both heaven and earth.
2) Because of this we are to go and make disciples, not just converts.

3) We are to make disciples of nations, not just individuals.
4) Disciples are students, and we make them disciples by teaching them.
5) Discipleship begins with baptism, which is the commitment to die with Him to our old self so that we may also walk in newness of life.
6) The discipleship continues with teaching them to observe ***all*** that He commanded.
7) This is what we are to do until the end of the age.

The reason we want to understand the times is so we can understand our own purpose in them. With the Great Commission our work is certainly cut out for us. Our goal should be to hear those great words on that great day when the Lord will judge the world, **"Well done good and faithful servant" (Matthew 25:21 NIV)** because we fulfilled His purpose in our generation. To do His will is the reason why we are on the earth at this time, and His will is for the Great Commission to be fulfilled. The last generation before His return will accomplish this.

Every Christian has a part to play in preparing the way for the Lord. A mighty force of apostles, prophets, evangelists, pastors, and teachers are being prepared for these times. The works that the Lord did, and even greater works, will be given to them to fulfill this great purpose (see John 14:12). There is an army being mobilized like the world has never seen, and before the end comes, the whole world will have seen them and heard their message. This is to give everyone the opportunity to prepare themselves for the coming kingdom.

If we are Christians then we have joined this great army. We no longer belong to ourselves, and we no longer live for ourselves, but for Him. We are soldiers of the cross. Let us not waste a single day of learning to use the weapons and armor that we have been given for this purpose, especially sharpening "the sword of the Spirit," which is the Word of God that has been given to us (see Ephesains 6:17). We are all going to get a chance to use it. By this we help build a bridge for this present world into the age to come—the kingdom of God on earth.

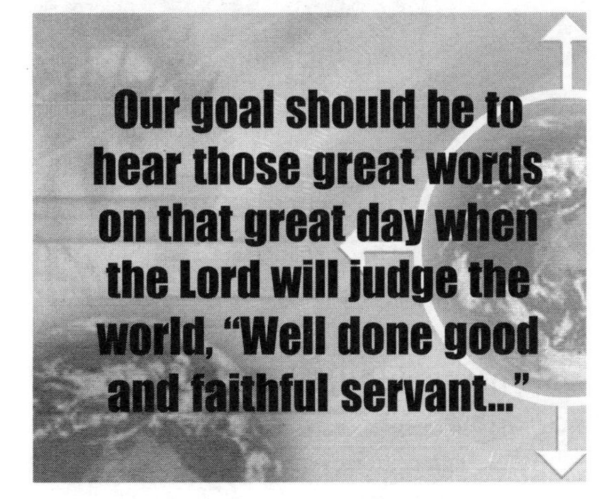

SUMMARY

Now, just as a compass has 360 degrees, there are many other lesser purposes which are nevertheless purposes of God for us. However, once you have the main cardinal points established it is much easier to find:

1) Where we are.
2) Where we are headed.
3) How to change our course if we are not headed in the right direction.

If we are headed in the right direction, Christ will be the center of our lives. This means that the compelling drive of our lives will be to know Him and serve Him by doing His will.

If we are living as we should live, our identity should be first and foremost who we are in Christ, not who we are in the world.

If we are headed in the right direction, even though the systems of this world are collapsing, we have a kingdom that cannot be shaken, which we will be building upon in peace with righteousness and justice.

If we are headed in the right direction, as the evil in man matures, with sin and evil becoming more pronounced as in the days of Noah, we will be growing in love, faith, and the fruits of the Spirit that counters that which is growing in the world.

If we are headed in the right direction, our lives will revolve around our mission—fulfilling the Great Commission, daily seeking to take more ground for the kingdom of God by revealing the glory of our King and His kingdom.

If we are living as we should live, our identity should be first and foremost who we are in Christ, not who we are in the world. By this I mean, if you think of yourself as an engineer, school teacher, or even mother or father first, we are not on course to be or to do what we are here for. This does not mean that these cannot be an identity, but if our identity is not first and foremost who we are in Christ, we are not on course, and the time is coming when we will almost certainly be "lost at sea," or lost with the rest of humanity.

That may sound alarmist, but make no mistake, as the Lord Jesus Himself warned when giving His main discourse about the end of the age:

"And because lawlessness is increased, most people's love will grow cold" (Matthew 24:12). He did not say here that this would happen to "some," or even "many," but that it will happen to "most." He then continues by saying, in the next verse, **"But the one who endures to the end, he shall be saved" (Matthew 24:12).**

Just the fact that you are reading this is an indication that you are a seeker of God. You may just be a casual seeker, or even an occasional seeker, which is certainly better than not being a seeker at all, but it will not be enough to keep you through the storms that are going to come upon the world. If there is anything in our lives that takes precedence over God, then it is an idol that has usurped His rightful place. If this is the case, for us to get on course He must be the main focus and greatest passion of our lives. Anything else is a diversion and deception from the true Christian life.

Good can be the worst enemy of best. Good can also be the worst enemy of God in our lives. It is right to be devoted to our family, our job, serving our neighbors through service organizations, etc. But if any of these eclipse God and service to Him as the main focus and devotion of our lives, then we have made idols of these otherwise good things.

To place anything above God in our lives also greatly reduces our effectiveness in the very good things that may have taken His place. Man was created to walk with God, and we simply do not function right without being properly united with Him. We may accomplish some things, but it will be far less and far inferior to what we could have accomplished when rightly related to Him. That is why we are told in Matthew 6:33, **"But seek first His kingdom and His righteousness, and all these things will be added to you."**

If we love God more than we love our family, we will love our family much more than we could otherwise. If we are walking in fellowship with God, obeying Him in all things, and abiding in Him so as to bear fruit, we will accomplish many times more what we could do for this world any other way.

If we are pursuing the Lord, seeking to do all that we do in obedience to Him, we are seeking His kingdom first. To seek His kingdom is to seek the place where He is King. If we are doing this, then everything else we need will be given to us. This is the solemn promise of God. We are foolish to want to do anything without Him.

If we are going to discern the truth of biblical prophecy, we must grasp that understanding His truth is not just a matter of getting our principles and formulas lined up right. His truth is a river of living water that gives life. His truth is not meant to just give us facts, but it is meant to change us, to become our life. Therefore, if we are pursuing His kingdom, and His righteousness, then He should be becoming King of more and more of our lives, and we should be growing in righteousness. Only then will our message of His kingdom have life in it.

So this is our pursuit—to understand the biblical prophecies of our times, not just to know them, but to be a part of God's purpose in them. Living in fellowship and obedience to God is the only foundation for true understanding. We do not really know the Way or the Truth if Jesus is not also our Life.

Determine you are going to seek to walk with Him in everything that you do. Seek His kingdom in all that you do by seeking His Lordship in it. If we are on course with our lives, His presence and His authority should be growing in everything we do. ■

It's Time to Dance with the King

by Joni Ames

It's time to dance with the King,
Let Him, His love impart;
Embrace Him closely, face to face,
Dance with Him, heart to heart.

It's time to dance with our King
And never look away;
In love forever, with a love
That's gaze will never stray.

We've danced too long the world's way
And kept step to its tune;
But no one else can love like Him
And cause our hearts to swoon.

Let's guard our hearts from all but Him,
His love is all complete;
Dancing in His strengthening arms,
Just let Him guide your feet.

Allow His love to light your path
And lead you in your ways;
For only He knows the road
And can, our hearts amaze.

I see Him reaching out to us
His scepter for this dance;
As He says, "Will you dance with Me
Inside each circumstance?"

"I'll teach to you the steps and moves,
And give you favor, sure;
I promise MY love will not leave,
But evermore endure."

"So will you let Me take your hand,
Let Me, your life, embrace?
Let Me, the lifter of your head,
Make all your pain erase?"

It's Time to Dance With the King

"Just follow close now, let ME lead,
As you rest safe from harm;
And from this desert I'll lead you,
As you lean on My Arm."

"I'll take away the heavy load
That you cannot endure;
As I sweep you from evil's grasp
Into My arms, secure."

It's time to dance now, with our King—
The King and Lord of all;
Reach out and take His hand today,
Responding to His call.

It's time to dance now with the King,
Let Him, His love impart;
Embrace Him closely, face to face,
Dance with Him, heart to heart.

It's time to dance now with our King,
And never look away;
In love forever, with a love
Which nevermore will stray.

All Scriptures are New King James Version.

The Power of Dreams

by John Paul Jackson

A dream's impact on our lives, and on the lives of those around us, can be profound. Dreams have caused kings to scour the earth for an interpretation. Nations have been conquered, inventions have been discovered, solutions have been found, and lives have been changed all because of these night parables called dreams.

My ministry changed radically after I had a dream several years ago. In the dream, I was experiencing stomach cramps. The pain was so intense that I went to a doctor. The doctor took out a stethoscope and listened to my abdomen.

"Oh my goodness," he exclaimed. "You're pregnant!"

"I can't be pregnant," I protested. "I'm a man!"

"There's no doubt about it," the doctor replied. "You're pregnant, and we need to deliver the baby right now. We will have to do a C-section on you."

The doctor took out a scalpel and cut open my belly. I didn't even have a chance to lie down! He pulled out the baby, proclaimed it healthy, handed it to a nurse, and closed my incision by stapling my stomach back together. It was the fastest—and probably strangest—Caesarian section imaginable.

I woke up, stunned by what I had just witnessed. I wrote down the dream and meditated on it until the Holy Spirit gave me the interpretation. I was pregnant with something, but only God could birth it. And I did not even know I was expecting!

Later, the Holy Spirit revealed that this "C-section" was actually a "See-section" where I would train a group of young prophetic people to "see" and hear God. These "children" would be healthy and vibrant, but needing the nurturing of a father.

Incredible Dreams

This is just a small snapshot of the power of a dream; many others exist throughout history. The inventor of the sewing machine, Elias Howe, received his idea after he dreamed of savages carrying spears with holes through their tips. At a lower point in his career, George Frideric Handel composed the musical masterpiece "Messiah" after hearing the music in a dream where he saw *"all of heaven before me and the Great God himself."* Robert Louis Stevenson wrote his legendary novel, *The Strange Case of Dr. Jekyll and Mr. Hyde,* after it was conceived in a dream. Danish physicist and Nobel Prize winner Niels Bohr proposed a revolutionary theory about atomic and molecular structure after having a dream. Calpurnia, the third wife of Roman ruler Julius Caesar, dreamed of her husband's death. Alarmed the next morning, she begged him to stay with her, but he ignored her plea. Hours later, he was dead, murdered by his friend Brutus.

Dreams are incredibly powerful if we know their meaning. A dream can change a person; it can change a family; it can change a community; it can even change a nation.

Once I had a dream where I was traveling up a river in a little boat. Alongside the boat swam a porpoise—but it had been cut in half! I woke up and wondered what such a strange dream could mean. As I sought the Lord, He told me: *"The church you're going to speak at tomorrow has had its purpose cut in half. I want you to speak words to restore it. The church has concentrated on the head of the fish, and not the tail—where the power is. The tail is where My power to move the 'porpoise' comes from."*

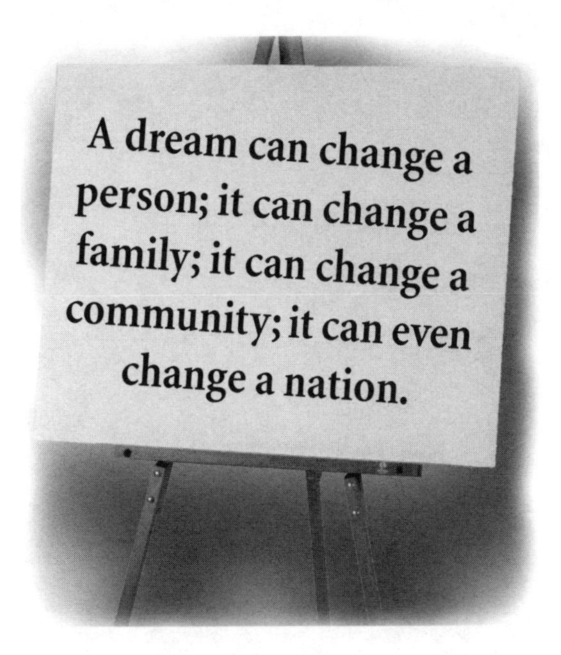

The Bible is full of examples of dreams like these which changed personal and communal destinies. Joseph's dreams as a young man were simple for him to interpret: Some day, my brothers will bow down before me. It took decades for that dream to be fulfilled, but it shaped his destiny.

Joseph's faith in God, and the power of dreams, led him to interpret dreams for others, even the most powerful man in the world at that time. When Joseph correctly identified God's message to Pharaoh, it changed the destiny of two nations: Egypt and Israel. Both were saved through the power of a dream.

Scripture tells us: **"For God may speak in one way, or in another, yet man does not perceive it. In a dream, in a vision of the night, when deep sleep falls upon men, while slumbering on their beds, then He opens the ears of men, and seals their instruction" (Job 33:14-16).**

> You would be surprised at the number of conservative leaders who are having intimate, powerful, inexplicable, and supernatural encounters with God.

Through the prophet Joel, God promised that He would give more and more dreams to His children in the last days. We are seeing that dramatic increase today.

The Value of Dreams

We sleep one-third of each day, which means we will spend one-third of our lives sleeping. By the time we are sixty years old, we will have spent twenty years asleep. This is twenty years God could have been speaking, but we did not perceive it. This is exactly what was written in Job 33:14-15, **"God may speak in one way, or in another, yet man does not perceive it. In a dream..."**

One-third of the Bible deals directly or indirectly with dreams and visions. And yet the Western church has been too willing to allow the fascinating and mysterious world of dreams to slip into the hands of the New Age. It is time to recapture what the New Age movement has stolen from the church! God wants to restore His awe to us and for that to happen, we must accept that God is the same today—still speaking to us in dreams and visions and amazing us with His supernatural power.

You would be surprised at the number of conservative leaders who are having intimate, powerful, inexplicable, and supernatural encounters with God. Sadly, many are reluctant to share their dreams and supernatural experiences in public, because they are afraid of losing their ministries. No wonder the New Age movement thinks the church is clueless to the power of God!

Several years ago, some of my interns noticed that many bookstores and coffeehouses were offering workshops on psychics, witchcraft, and other New Age phenomena to lure people into their shops. One intern approached a bookstore manager and told her that he could interpret dreams. Intrigued, the manager immediately tested him by sharing several dreams, which he interpreted. She was so impressed that the manager scheduled a dream interpretation event for customers the following week—on the slowest night of the week. Later, she was stunned when sales shot through the roof on that night.

It is exciting to bring God's light into otherwise dark places. Along the way, we have made a shocking discovery. Nearly one-third of those whose dreams we interpret are Christians who have naively embraced psychic experiences, due to their hunger for the supernatural. When their local church failed to address their need to be awed by God's power, these individuals searched outside the church to meet the hunger of their spirit. Sadly, many were lured to the dark side of spiritual power.

Today, the occult and New Age movement are feeding our culture's appetite for spiritual power. God continues to give people dreams, often warning them not to go down a certain dark path. But instead of turning to Him, these people often look elsewhere for the interpretation to their dreams.

Numerous people have given their lives to the Lord after hearing a dream's interpretation. Something inside their heart affirms the dream's meaning that we offer them. Tears begin to roll down many of their faces; each one is powerfully touched. Most open up and eagerly want to share more dreams. As they share their dreams, the prophetic Spirit of God begins to unlock their hearts. Often they ask, "How did you know these things?"

People are created with a capacity to dream. God opens the doors, preparing people's hearts to respond to what the Father is doing. Through biblical dream interpretation, God is touching lives in profound ways.

We should not be surprised by this desperate hunger that we see in our culture today. Nebuchadnezzar had a dream in Daniel 2 and ordered his advisors to be put to death when they failed to interpret it. Only Daniel could solve the mystery of the mighty king's dream. Similarly, none of Egypt's wise men could interpret Pharaoh's dream of the fourteen cows. But Joseph, a prisoner, could, and he was rewarded by being made second-in-command of the entire nation. People are thirsty for interpretations.

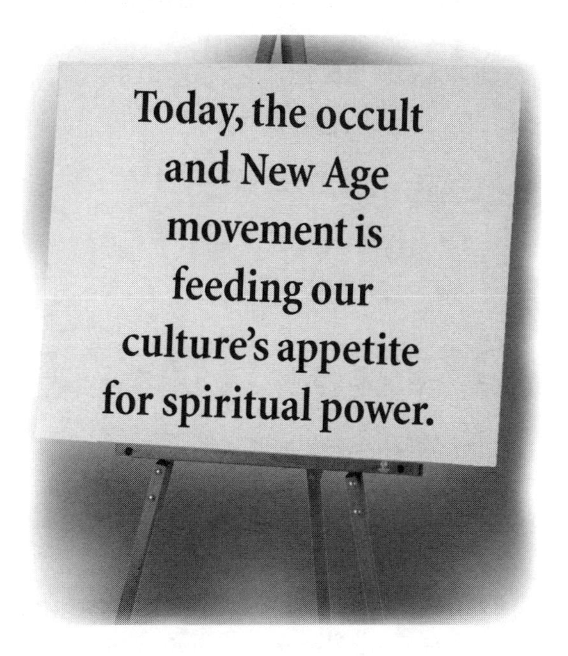

I believe Christians should take time to meditate and study the dreams recorded in the Bible. Why not consider these passages: Genesis 20:2-8, Genesis 28:11-18, Genesis 31:9-14, Genesis 31:23-31, Genesis 37:4-21, Genesis 40:4-23, Genesis 41:1-36, Judges 7:13-15, 1 Kings 3:4-15, Daniel 2:1-49, Daniel 4:4-37, Matthew 1:18-25, Matthew 2:7-23, and Matthew 27:15-24.

By contemplating the mysteries of these dreams and their interpretations, we lay the foundation for a biblical method of dream interpretation. None of these dreams can be interpreted properly by using the modern New Age schools of interpretation. Freud, Jung, or Gestalt could not arrive at God's meaning of these dreams using their techniques. That's why we must build our familiarity with God's symbolic language recorded in the Bible.

> It is not uncommon for God to give a dream to non-Christians to draw them closer to Him.

Daniel sought the Lord for wisdom in interpreting dreams, solving riddles, and explaining spiritual mysteries. In fact, Scripture says that among all the astrologers, seers, psychics, and magicians in Babylon, none had more spiritual insight than Daniel (see Daniel 1:17-21). Everyone noticed his keen insight—even those with great authority (see Daniel 5:11-13). A Babylonian king was so impressed by Daniel's understanding of dreams that he promoted Daniel to a high-ranking position in the land (see Daniel 5:29). Thanks to the power of the Holy Spirit, we can have the same influence on people today.

Another way of learning God's language is to write down our own dreams, pray about them, and mediate on them. What is God showing you through your dreams? What mysteries has He hidden in your sleep for you to discover?

A dream journal is a wonderful way to chronicle the insights God whispers during the night. By keeping a dream journal, you will be able to see God's faithfulness in guiding you through life. Threads of his involvement will become evident as you live and move and have your being in Him (see Acts17:28).

When we commit to recording our dreams, I have noticed that God increases the number of dreams we have. He honors our inquiry and interest in studying our dreams by unfolding more spiritual insight. His Holy Spirit helps us to understand the deep things of God.

As Christians become more and more comfortable with dream interpretation, many begin praying that their unsaved friends and loved ones would have dreams that confound them. It is not uncommon for God to give dreams to non-Christians to draw them closer to Him.

My passion for dream evangelism is strong. Once I dreamed that a thousand people a day would come to the Lord because they had a dream interpreted by a Christian. I believe that dreams are a key battlefield in the coming war against darkness. The New Age movement wants this arena, but God is offering it to us. We must begin to pray for opportunities to interpret the dreams of non-Christians, and then, ask God to equip us for this monumental task. ■

Entering Another Dimension

by Steve Thompson

Just over one hundred years ago, two bicycle mechanics from the Midwestern United States embarked on a quest that changed the modern world. They developed the ability to leave the two dimensions that mankind had previously traveled in and found their way into "the heavens." The story of how two uneducated, untrained, and unlikely men changed the world by discovering the secrets that led to powered flight is a tremendous message to the church in our generation.

Through patient, persistent, dogged pursuit, Wilbur and Orville Wright discovered the way for mankind to enter the heavens at will. And this accurately reflects the calling before the church today—to discover how to access the heavenly realm, and move in the powers of the age to come at will. Although this may seem extreme at first glance, consider this prophecy which Jesus spoke about those who believed on Him:

> **"Truly, truly, I say to you, he who believes in Me, the works that I do shall he do also; and greater works than these shall he do; because I go to the Father" (John 14:12).**

Although many have attempted to rationalize how this Scripture will be fulfilled, it will be fulfilled just as Jesus spoke it—by individuals, who like Him, are able to manifest the kingdom of God as the need arises. But there is a process of discovering, testing, refinement, and attainment that enables this fulfillment. And the story of Wilbur and Orville Wright is a poignant, prophetic picture of how we can discover the secrets of God and access "the heavenly realm."

Inspired During Failure

Orville and Wilbur Wright became interested in flight as children. Their father, a bishop in the United Church of the Brethren, gave them a toy helicopter when they were young. Both Wilbur and Orville were fascinated with the idea that man might be able to fly. However, like most people, their fascination dwindled as they grew older and became engaged in trying to make a living.

Although many had attempted to create different crafts to ride the wind, apparently no one had addressed this issue of controlling their craft in the air.

Years later after the brothers had developed a successful business repairing and building bicycles, their interest in flight was rekindled. In the mid 1890s, a number of scientists, adventurers, and engineers across the globe were attempting to develop a craft that would enable men to fly. Samuel Langley, Otto Lilienthal, and Octave Chanute were a few of the more renowned men making these attempts.

In August 1896, as some of these men were having modest success in very short glider flights, a tragedy occurred. The world's greatest glider pilot, Otto Lilienthal, died from injuries sustained in a crash in Germany. With his death, many who had begun believing that human flight was possible began retreating and retracting their claims.

Lilienthal had completed hundreds of glider flights. He was an accomplished athlete, as were most glider pilots, but was also scientifically motivated. He had established an organized table of flight data that many were using in their attempts to fly. At his death, the media and many engineers declared that human flight was impractical and probably impossible. Major newspapers featured articles mocking those who attempted flight.

The tragic death of Lilienthal was the catalyst which reignited Wilbur and Orville Wright's interest in human flight. Wilbur soon began reading everything available on flight. As he studied, he developed the hypothesis that Lilienthal had died not because flight was impossible, but due to his inability to maneuver the glider in flight.

Although many had attempted to create different crafts to ride the wind, apparently no one had addressed this issue of controlling their craft in the air. The identification of this problem provided Wilbur and his brother with a goal they believed was attainable and necessary—the development of controlled, powered human flight.

Radical, Unreasonable Vision

Wilbur and Orville Wright were not trained as scientists or engineers; they repaired and built bicycles for a living. Considering the state of technology in the late 1890s, it is remarkable that they were convinced they could produce an airplane at that time. The technology of the day was so primitive that the bicycle had only been made safe in the previous ten years.

Prior to this time, only the most athletic could ride bicycles (with the extremely large front wheel and very small rear one) because they were so difficult to balance. Someone came up with the idea to build a bicycle with two wheels of equal size and to sync them together with a chain and sprockets on each wheel. Thus the "safety bicycle" was invented and soon cycling or "wheeling" was a national craze in America.

In this environment where the bicycle had just become safe, the Wright brothers decided to pursue the creation of powered, controlled, human flight. They had a radical and almost unreasonable vision. The logical next step should have been to pursue the development of the motorcycle or the perfection of the automobile. The Wright brothers, however, completely bypassed these more reasonable steps and aimed for the skies.

Afflicted with Faith

It is almost a misnomer to say the Wright brothers chose to pursue flight—a better description is they were chosen to pursue it. Wilbur was inspired by a belief so consuming that he described it as an affliction. He was publicly quoted as saying, *"I am convinced that human flight is both possible and practical."* Privately Wilbur revealed that his conviction was more than a choice.

> *"For some years I have been afflicted with the belief that flight is possible to man. My disease has increased in severity and I feel that it will soon cost me an increased amount of money if not my life."*

In this environment where the bicycle had just become safe, the Wright brothers decided to pursue the creation of powered, controlled, human flight.

As Wilbur read and thought about the problems associated with flight, a deep conviction of the possibilities consumed him. He had made a choice to pursue his interest, but soon it began pursuing him. He could not escape the conviction which gripped his heart and mind—flight was both possible and practical.

Wilbur believed that something which had never been done could be done, which was sustained, controlled human flight. He also believed that he and Orville could accomplish it—in spite of having no training, experience, or clear pathway for starting their pursuit.

Overcoming Traditional, Religious Objections

With Lilienthal's death, the objections to human flight that had been simmering in some arenas now boiled over. The prevailing objection was religiously themed, *"If God had meant for man to fly, He would have given him wings."* This sentiment had an appearance of humility because it pretended to acknowledge God's sovereignty. But this idea was not born of humility, it was merely an excuse to justify the failure that everyone was experiencing.

Wilbur and Orville Wright were humble enough to learn from others, but also confident enough to analyze their successes and failures as well.

Wilbur had other ideas however. He believed in looking for what was not clearly seen. Just because mankind was not anatomically enabled for flight, did not mean God had not intended for him to fly. God had provided other means to get mankind airborne, including faith, intellect, perseverance, and ingenuity. Wilbur and Orville Wright realized that faith was not needed for the obvious but for seeing the invisible realm and accessing it. They began pursuing the secrets of flight that they realized must have been hidden from others in the past.

Studying to Show Themselves Approved

Wilbur baptized himself in the existing knowledge of flight development, even though that knowledge had never produced what they pursued. He realized that although no one had successfully demonstrated controlled or powered flight, there had been truths learned through both the partial successes and the failures of those who had gone before them.

Wilbur and Orville Wright were humble enough to learn from others, but also confident enough to analyze their successes and failures as well. This confidence was remarkable, considering they had still never flown. This problem solving approach was born of their practical experience in business, and nothing else. They were not judging the efforts of others in order to criticize them; they were analyzing successes and failures, so they could learn and improve.

In addition to reading everything available on flight, Wilbur began corresponding with other inventors. He also studied animals that were anatomically suited for flight. He studied birds, insects, and other flying animals in books and in their natural habitats.

God Breathed on Their Study

As the Wright brothers gave themselves to studying flight, God breathed on their efforts. While observing buzzards flying near his home, the thought flashed upon

Wilbur's soul that birds, while flying, adjusted the tips of their wings, one at a positive angle, and the other at a negative angle, which effectively turned the bird into a living windmill. He also hypothesized that the birds reversed their wing angles when necessary. This enabled them to adapt to any change or shift in the wind.

Wilbur dubbed this concept "wing warping." He and Orville began sketching ideas about how to warp the wings of a glider. However, everything they thought of or projected seemed too heavy or complex to be practical. Although their ideas were correct, they could not find a way to implement them practically.

Young Men Had Visions

One day, as he was repairing a bicycle, Wilbur was mulling over the different problems associated with adjusting wing angles. As he thought over the problem and his seeming inability to solve it, he absentmindedly began twisting a cardboard box that had contained an inner tube.

He noticed that when he twisted the box, one end turned up while the other turned down. This mirrored the "wing warping" concept he conjectured the birds employed. As he looked at the cardboard box, in his mind's eye, the sides of the box became the two wings of a biplane. Wilbur almost immediately saw how he could craft a system that would warp the wings of a plane.

Within days the brothers had built a biplane kite and fitted it with light cables that caused the wing warping to occur simultaneously. They also fitted it with a moveable tail to control the pitch of the kite. When Wilbur and Orville tested it, the kite worked perfectly.

Not Skipping Ahead

The Wright brothers had solved their first riddle, but at this point they had not created a working airplane, they had only flown a nice kite. Their theory had proven correct in a small scale test, but their vision was for developing flight, not just flying theories.

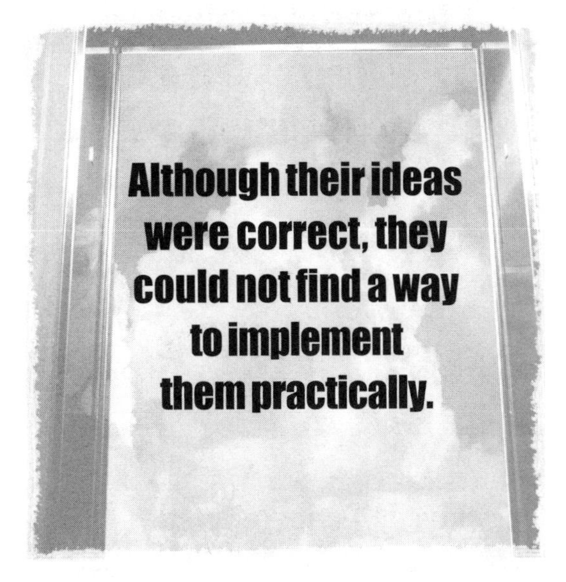

After their biplane kite was successful, they took the next step and crafted a biplane glider. They employed the same wing warping technology, experimenting with different schemes related to the tail of the plane. They tried their glider both with and without the tails to see the different effect on control, including pitch.

The Wright brothers did not skip any steps in their process of pursuing flight. They were painfully patient and methodical in their pursuit and implementation. When researching the best places for attempting glider flights, they performed detailed research on weather patterns, wind currents, and even soil density to ensure landings as soft as possible. The amount of research they engaged is staggering to our minds. Although they were attempting to develop flight, it was built on small steps, not gigantic leaps.

Instead of dabbling in their passion while earning a living, they lived their passion and dabbled in earning a living.

They Lived Unencumbered

Because their pursuit of flight was so tedious and time consuming, Wilbur and Orville had to make hard choices about their business and how to spend their greatest resource—time. Wilbur once wrote to another would-be aviator that he had considered and was dealing with this issue:

> *I have been trying to arrange my affairs in such a way that I can devote my entire time for a few months to experiment in this field.*

Instead of dabbling in their passion while earning a living, they lived their passion and dabbled in earning a living. They arranged their lives so they could devote themselves to developing flight relatively unencumbered. They brought another man in to do the majority of their mechanical work and their sister Katherine took over the management of their business.

Overcoming Difficulties and Depression

As the Wright brothers moved further into the glider phase of their experiments, they were both encouraged and confused. Their glider did fly, but often lost altitude in turns and failed to generate the lift they had expected. They also found that the controls worked, but overall the glider was cumbersome and not as responsive as they had projected. Their ideas were working, but not well enough to move to the next stage.

During this season Wilbur had begun corresponding with Octave Chanute, another engineer who was well respected in the budding field of aeronautics. Chanute asked Wilbur if he could join them in Kitty Hawk, North Carolina, where they had chosen to test their glider, to observe some of their flight attempts. Here the Wright brothers experienced some of their most difficult days.

Again, their glider failed to perform to their expectations. Although they set the record for longest length for a glider flight, they were severely disappointed. So much so, that Wilbur eventually declared to Orville on their return trip to Ohio, *"Not within one thousand years would man ever fly."* Wilbur then dejectedly confided to Orville that his flying days were probably over.

Challenging Conventional, Accepted Doctrines

Although the Wright brothers were discouraged, Octave Chanute was impressed. In the middle of 1901, he invited Wilbur to address the Society of Western Engineers and give a report on their experiments in flight. However, Wilbur was so despondent over their mixed results that he decided against accepting the invitation. It was only through the cajoling encouragement of his sister Katherine that he decided to accept the invitation. So Wilbur now had to prepare a paper and speech to address the group.

As he poured over his data from their past few years of flight experiments, he came to a stunning conclusion. He decided that based on their projections and their glider flights, the scientific data that had been compiled by the late hero Lilienthal had to be incorrect. At that time, almost all scientists and engineers accepted Lilienthal's tables of lift and drag without question, but Wilbur was set to challenge them in his speech. When he did, remarkably, his thoughts found great acceptance among these engineers.

Renewed by the reception of his speech, he and Orville set out to determine accurate tables of lift and drag. To compile a list of data for these tables, they created a wind tunnel out of spare bicycle parts and tediously measured the lift created by different wing shapes and lengths. In this laboratory setting, they discovered some surprising facts.

After months of tedious testing in their wind tunnel, the Wright brothers created a newer, more aerodynamically sound glider, which had greater lift than their original model.

First, Lilienthal's data was fairly accurate. However, a factor he used in calculating lift and drag was drastically off the mark. This factor, the *coefficient of air pressure* had been identified almost 150 years earlier by a British scientist and was commonly "accepted as the gospel." But it was way off the mark. This accounted for the lack of lift that their gliders had experienced. They also found that Lilienthal's wing shapes were fairly inefficient as well and could be dramatically improved.

Doing Whatever Is Necessary

After months of tedious testing in their wind tunnel, the Wright brothers created a newer, more aerodynamically sound glider, which had greater lift than their original model. With the lift issue settled, they could now address the issue of better control in flight. Toward the end of 1902, their third glider became the first airplane with functional controls for maneuvering in all three dimensions.

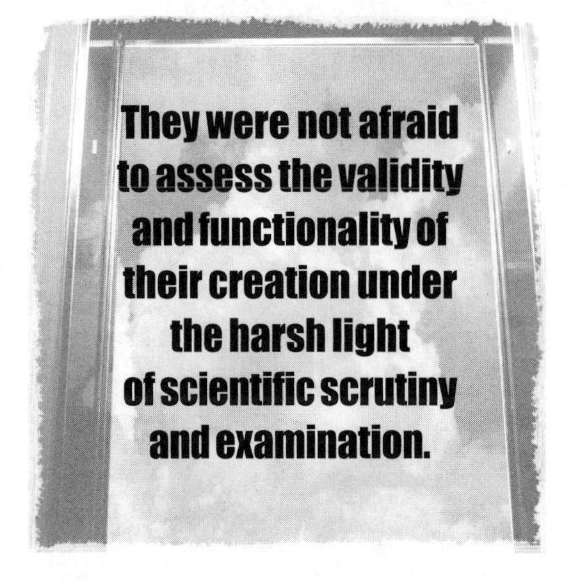

Soon, the brothers were ready to add a power source to their flyer. Contacting more than twenty different companies, they requested an engine powerful enough yet light enough for their airplane. Every company they contacted refused. Undaunted, the brothers spent a couple of months building their own engine with the help of the mechanic who was handling most of their bicycle business now.

They also had to design and build a propeller that would work with their plane. They built and tested numerous propellers until they crafted one that produced the amount of power they deemed necessary for their Wright Flyer to get airborne. This entailed many more hours, failures, and adjustments, but it also meant many more discoveries and successes.

They Analyzed Their Failures Unemotionally

The Wright brothers were not afraid of the truth. They were moved by inspiration and by faith. They saw the invisible realm and attempted to implement it in the real world. But they also analyzed the efficacy of their visions and faith. They were not afraid to assess the validity and functionality of their creation under the harsh light of scientific scrutiny and examination.

Wilbur and Orville were not concerned about their reputation—they were interested in creating flight. They were not concerned with being right in the eyes of others—they wanted to be better at what they were attempting. Their vision was not just to get into the air, but to be able to function there for sustained lengths of time—only theories which actually worked would support them.

A Heart of Wonder

The Wright brothers were remarkable men. They were dreamers *and* engineers. They had prophetic insight, but used practical hindsight to evaluate all of their theories. While they excelled at problem solving, they were propelled forward by joy and the passion of discovering the hidden secrets of the universe. Wilbur had written to another experimenter in 1903:

> *Isn't it astonishing that all of these secrets have been preserved for so many years so that we could discover them!*

Wilbur was driven by the joy of discovering the secrets that would enable them to rise above the earth. This heart of childlike wonder and excitement, enthralled with unraveling the mysteries of our universe, sustained him through the tedium and failures they experienced. And they experienced more failure in their pursuit of flight than most could have endured and still continued.

Accessing the Heavens

After traveling to North Carolina in the autumn of 1903, the Wrights spent several months preparing everything for their attempt at flight. They built a new hanger for their flyer. They built a track that would guide their powered take-off from a level starting point. They made their plans and rechecked all of their calculations. They were soon ready to fly.

Eventually the perfect day for flying arrived, but the Wright brothers did not attempt to fly their craft. The perfect day turned out to be a Sunday, and they had promised their father, the bishop, that they would honor the Lord by honoring the Sabbath. It must have been difficult for them to sit idle, instead of launching their craft, but this decision proved to be wise for practical reasons as well.

Over the next days the weather grew stormier and windier than would be completely safe. However, the brothers decided they needed to try their wings in less than optimal conditions for personal reasons—they wanted to be home for Christmas. As they would later discover, if they had attempted flight that previous Sunday, they probably would have been unsuccessful. They would later realize some of their calculations were incorrect and they needed the extra wind.

On December 17, 1903, a storm was brewing. The wind was howling and the clouds were gathering. But now the Wright brothers threw caution to the wind. They and the North Carolinians who had promised to help them began to set up the equipment to get their flyer airborne.

The perfect day turned out to be a Sunday, and they had promised their father, the bishop, that they would honor the Lord by honoring the Sabbath.

They made four attempts that day and each became more successful than the previous. They were awkward and halting according to our standards, but for the first time in human history, mankind entered the sky from a level starting point and traveled through the air. Man had entered into the heavenly realm. Life on this planet would never be the same.

A Prophetic Picture

Their most successful flight that day covered more than 850 feet and lasted almost one minute. Later that day, a gust caught the flyer as they were moving it, and completely smashed it to bits, while flipping over a coworker who became entangled in the cables. That original flyer would never fly again, but the Wright brothers' spirits could not be dampened.

There is no qualification required to discover these secrets other than the patient, persistent pursuit of God and His kingdom.

Over the next two years, the Wrights refined and reworked their flyers, until they had produced the world's first practical airplane in 1905. This plane could stay airborne thirty minutes at a time and was fully maneuverable. It is said that until the Wright brothers, no one did anything fundamentally right in aeronautics, and after them no one has done anything fundamentally different.

All current airplanes, satellites, and even the space shuttle function on the discoveries that were made by these two brothers from Ohio. They literally changed the way that we experience our world. What the Wright brothers accomplished was arguably one of the greatest pursuits and discoveries in history.

What they did in the natural realm, we are called to do in the spiritual realm. We are called to discover the secrets of accessing the heavenly realm and to move in the powers of the age to come. Their passion, their pursuit, and their process are a picture of how we can fulfill our calling.

There are secrets to moving in greater power and spiritual authority. God has concealed these secrets for those who are hungry and passionate enough to pursue Him and them. There is no qualification required to discover these secrets other than the patient, persistent pursuit of God and His kingdom.

The book of wisdom says, **"It is the glory of God to conceal a matter, but the glory of kings is to search out a matter" (Proverbs 25:2).** God has issued an invitation not by revealing His secrets, but by hiding them. However He hides them *for* us, not *from* us. The conviction that something is available, even though we cannot see it, is our invitation to join this quest.

Our response to this invitation is the ongoing pursuit of discovery and attainment. Our call is to seek God and His kingdom until we consistently move in the power and spiritual authority that some in previous generations only accessed intermittently. Just as the Wright brothers discovered the "secrets of the heavens" and developed practical powered flight, we too are called to discover how to move in the "heavenly realm" just as Jesus did. ■

A Glorious FUTURE

by Rick Joyner

Hebrews 6:11 declares, **"And we desire that each one of you show the same diligence so as to realize the full assurance of hope until the end."** In contrast to this, many, if not most of the teachings on the last days are filled with doom. Hope is the foundation of the true knowledge of prophecy, not fear. God, with His goodness, righteousness, and justice will prevail in all ways over the darkness that has enveloped this earth.

Any eschatology which focuses on doom instead of the glorious promises has fundamentally misunderstood the prophecies of the end times. Certainly there will be troubles, even the greatest time of trouble that the world has ever known. Even so, troubles are not the main point! In fact, they are not even worthy of a side show. We are coming to the time of the greatest revelation of the glory of God that the world has ever known. That is the main point.

Neither are Christians doomed at the end of the age. We are coming to the time when Christians will prosper as never before. They will walk in the power, provision, and glory of God in a way so spectacular that Israel's deliverance from Egypt was only a "shadow" of the reality to come. There will be a distinction made between those who live in "Goshen" and those who worship the idols of this world. Just as Israel left Egypt with its treasures, the wealth of the wicked is being stored up for the righteous.

However, just as Israel was not immediately taken to the closest shopping mall to spend their new found wealth, but rather into the wilderness so they could use it to build a dwelling place for God, it will be the same for us. The wealth of the nations is not coming to us so we can live luxuriously, but so we can build God a dwelling place to live among us. This is for the building up of the body of Christ, His church, His dwelling place. The presence of the Lord among us is a far more wonderful thing than all of the luxuries of this earth could ever be.

MANY YEARS AGO, SEVERAL PROPHETIC FRIENDS AND MYSELF WERE ALL SHOWN THAT ALMOST THE ENTIRE LEADERSHIP OF THE CHURCH AT THAT TIME WAS DEVOID OF THE TRUE GIFT OF DISCERNMENT.

We cannot understand what the Lord is doing on the earth without understanding His most basic purpose for the earth, which is what Peter called the **"...restoration of all things" (Acts 3:21).** We know His first priority is the restoration of His temple, the church, so that He can dwell among us. However, the church is not the whole purpose of God, but it is a means, the vehicle through which He intends to restore all things that were lost by the Fall. The earth, and all it contains, is the Lord's, and will be restored.

The Nature of Discernment

One of the main goals in our gaining knowledge of the times is the process of our growing in discernment. The true gift of discernment is a gift that we are certainly going to need in the times ahead. Many years ago, several prophetic friends and myself were all shown that almost the entire leadership of the church at that time was devoid of the true gift of discernment. This does not mean they did not have discernment, but they lacked the gift of discernment, which is a supernatural gift that transcends human wisdom, or what we may call "street knowledge." The Lord also made it clear to us that this gift was one of which we were all going to need in the times ahead. He not only wanted to give it to His leaders, but to all of His people.

It was very soon after this that another prophetic friend of mine, Bob Jones, was shown by the Lord that the church was being continually misled by "a false gift of discernment." He said a "spirit of suspicion" was masquerading as the gift of discernment in the church, and hardly anyone recognized it. He was then told that the true gift of discernment could only work through compassion, and He had given him Philippians 1:9 as the Scripture for it, **"And this I pray, that your love may abound still more and more in real knowledge and all discernment."** The Lord went on to tell him that "anything but love will distort discernment."

My way of thinking at the time was that "love is blind," more prone to cloud your discernment of a person rather than help you to discern accurately. However, the Lord said that the opposite was true. As I sought the Lord on this matter, He showed me over and over how suspicion had caused me to misunderstand many people, and how I had often missed His will in matters because of it.

The Nature of Spiritual Authority

It was at this time that the Lord began to speak to some of us about how all true spiritual authority is founded upon love. We see this in the Lord's own walk on the earth. It was when He had compassion for the sheep that were without a shepherd that He became their Shepherd. It was when He had compassion on those who sat in darkness that He became their Teacher.

I was then shown that I would know when He was sending me because I would feel His love for those to whom I was being sent. I would know that I was being sent to a church when I started to feel His love for that church. I would know that I was being sent to a ministry when I started to feel His love for that ministry. The same is true for a city, a country, a culture, or a people group. It was only through this love that I would be able to discern the roots of their problems and bondage so that I could help them.

Truly loving someone does not mean that you will only see the good in them. It means that you can see them as they are and only seek good for them. It is for this reason that Paul wrote in II Corinthians 5:14, **"For the love of Christ controls us..."** This leads us to one of those ultimate questions. What would we be like if the love of Christ was controlling all of our thoughts and actions? Then add to this the power of Christ abiding in us to do the works He did, and even greater works. What would our days be like if this were true?

THIS LEADS US TO ONE OF THOSE ULTIMATE QUESTIONS. WHAT WOULD WE BE LIKE IF THE LOVE OF CHRIST WAS CONTROLLING ALL OF OUR THOUGHTS AND ACTIONS?

There will be a people who walk the earth before this age is over about whom this will be true. They will have His love in them and will therefore walk the earth like He did. As we will see, this is sound, biblical prophecy concerning the end of this age.

Because our goal for knowing the Lord's will is to be prepared to do His will, let us be even more practical. What would you do today if His love was controlling you and His power was in you? Who would you heal? What devils would you cast out? For whom would you multiply their food? To whom would you preach the gospel of the kingdom?

WE ARE COMING TO THE TIME WHEN WE ARE GOING TO SEE HIS LOVE DEMONSTRATED THROUGH HIS PEOPLE, AND IT WILL COME WITH THE POWER OF HIS LOVE TO HELP PEOPLE.

We might also add some other practical questions to this. Would we have watched the television programs we did? How much of that gossip would we have even listened to, much less helped to spread? Would we have become that angry with our neighbor over such a small thing? Would we have gloated over the misfortune which struck a person whom we do not like, or would we even dislike them?

A most important, eternal truth is now being restored to the church. This truth is the truth of the power of the cross. This is going to change everything. It is even going to change us. There is nothing that reveals the love of God, or the power of God, like the cross. We are coming to the time when we are going to see His love demonstrated through His people, and it will come with the power of His love to help people. The cross is the power of God that is the answer to every human problem, and we are going to begin to see this. This is the **"full assurance of hope" (Hebrews 6:11)** that will keep us right to the end. ■

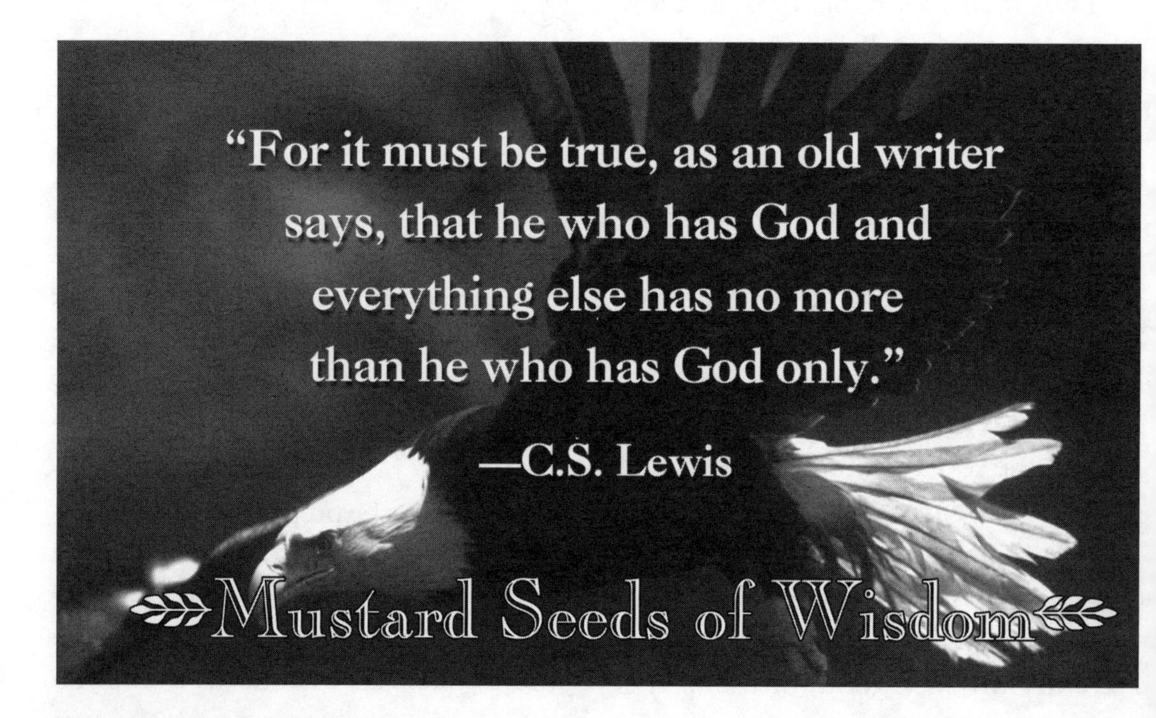

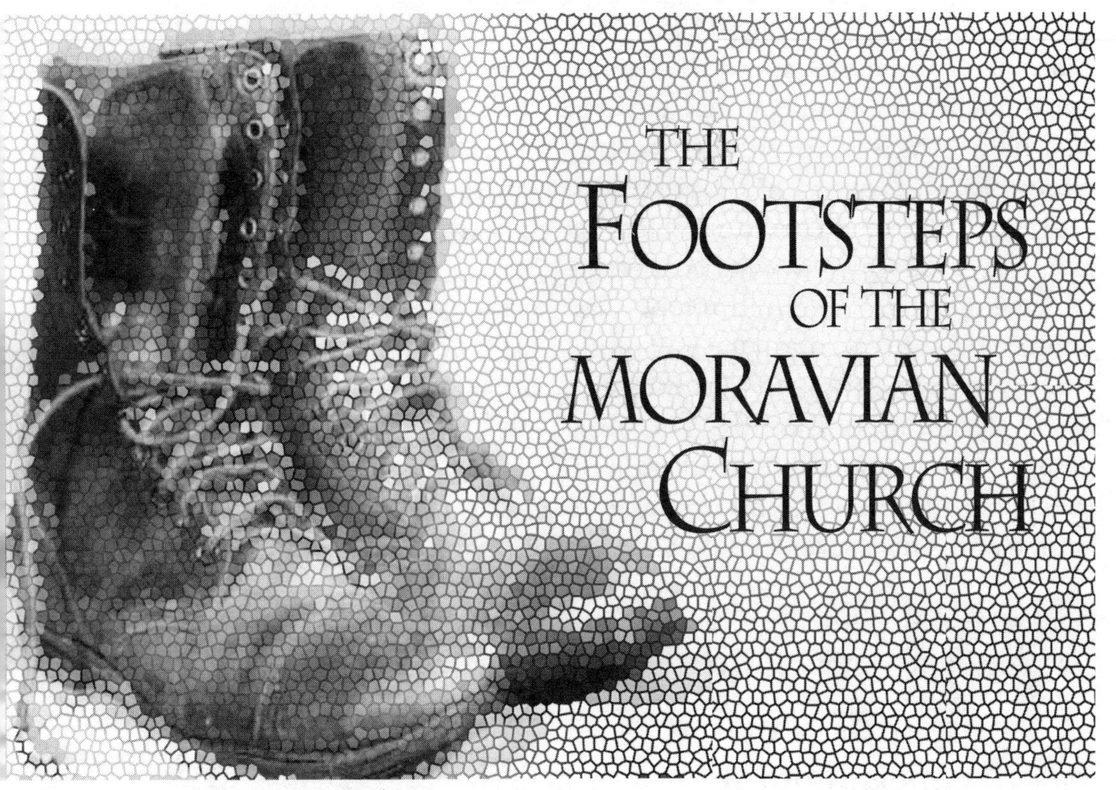

THE FOOTSTEPS OF THE MORAVIAN CHURCH

All Scriptures are King James Version.

by Pitts Evans

The Moravians first came to my attention as a group that had somehow influenced the life of Reformer, and Methodist founder, John Wesley. I later discovered that they had actually been instrumental in his salvation experience and had greatly impacted his ministry. The group again caught my eye because of a beautiful spot in the mountains of North Carolina known as Moravian Falls. Several dear friends told me that there seemed to be an abiding presence of God at Moravian Falls and in the surrounding area. When speaking of the spiritual climate of this area of North Carolina, they used the term "open heaven" to indicate the purity of the very atmosphere itself. As I began to make mental notes on this group, I found their footsteps in many unexpected places, both historically and geographically.

We will attempt to trace the spiritual roots and history of the Moravian Church, beginning with their origins in Europe and follow them to their settlements in America. As we trace their spiritual history, we must discuss the powerful impact and influence of Count Nikolaus von Zinzendorf. We will examine the foundations of their theology along with their influence on secular and church history. It is also our intention to look at their amazing chapter in the history of world missions. We will conclude with Moravian Falls and the possible reasons for God to be unusually accessible there.

GENERAL HISTORY OF THE MORAVIAN CHURCH

Many sources tell us that Count von Zinzendorf founded the Moravian

Church between 1727 and 1745.[1] The Moravians themselves say that their spiritual history began much earlier. The name "Moravian" identifies the place of the church's origin as Moravia in Europe. This area, including Bohemia, was located in what is now the Czech Republic. The entire region was converted to Christianity in the mid-ninth century by two Greek Orthodox missionaries, Cyril and Methodius. The area gradually came under the jurisdiction of the Roman Catholic Church over the course of the next several centuries.[2]

By the early sixteenth century, the Moravian Church numbered at least 200,000 members.

The Moravians credit the great Czech reformer, John Hus (1369-1415), for being the man who brought them back to spiritual independence from Rome.[3] The pre-Reformation church leader Hus, preached justification by faith, and the supreme authority of Scripture over a century before Martin Luther posted his 95 Thesis in 1517.[4] Like Luther, Hus sought sweeping reform in the universal Catholic Church. Unlike Luther, who died in his bed, Hus was burned at the stake as a heretic in 1415 for his reformation efforts.

Within fifty years after his death, the remnants of the followers of John Hus began to call themselves the Unitas Fratrum (*Unity of Brethren*).[5] The Moravian Church has been officially known as the Unitas Fratrum since 1457.[6] Though heavily persecuted, this group remained committed to the principals of reform that Hus had advocated. They remained active throughout their native Moravia and Bohemia from the initial founding of their movement. This makes the Unitas Fratrum/Moravians the oldest and longest continuing Reformation church. They predate the Lutheran Church by more than sixty years.[7] Historians have variously referred to this remnant, Moravian group as "Hussites," "Unity of Brethren," "United Brethren," "Bohemian Brethren," "Moravian Brethren," or more commonly as the Moravian Church.

By the early sixteenth century, the Moravian Church numbered at least 200,000 members. They had also provided the people of Bohemia and Moravia with the Bible in their own native languages. Persecution in 1547 led to a partial migration and church expansion into Poland. During these

[1] Note: The 1727 date refers to their famous prayer meeting of May 12, 1727 and the 1745 date refers to the date they were officially recognized as a church in Germany.

[2] Moravian Church in America, (online paper, 2003) www.moravian.org/history., p. 1.

[3] Ibid.

[4] Eddie L. Hyatt, *2000 Years of Charismatic Christianity*, (Dallas, 1998), p.103.

[5] Robert P. Gwinn, Chair, *The New Encyclopaedia Britannica, Micro. Vol. 8,* (Chicago, 1990), p. 310.

[6] Moravian, org/history, p. 1

[7] Hyatt, p. 103.

difficult years the church was forced to exist underground. It continued to grow and was eventually led by Bishop John Amos Comenius (1592-1670). The underground nature of the Unitas Fratrum/Moravian Church caused Comenius to refer to it as his beloved "hidden seed."[8] They survived the ravages of The Thirty Year War and The Peace of Westphalia Treaty in 1648, but were forced to continue as a persecuted, underground movement.[9]

COUNT NIKOLAUS LUDWIG GRAF VON ZINZENDORF

The hunted and persecuted Moravians fled to Protestant areas of Germany in the early 1700s. A group of these spiritual refugees settled on the estate of Count von Zinzendorf in 1722. Zinzendorf was born May 26, 1700 and died May 9, 1760. He was the son of an Austrian nobleman. His father died and his mother remarried while he was a very young child. He was brought up by his devout Pietist grandmother, the Baroness von Gersdorf.[10]

At the age of ten, Zinzendorf was sent away to study at Halle under the great Lutheran Pietist, August Francke (1663-1727).[11] His religious training was also deeply influenced by the writings of Pietist theologian and Lutheran pastor, Phillip Spener. Pietism was a spiritual renewal movement that was primarily seeking to revitalize German Lutheranism. It emphasized the study of Scripture, holy living or "pietism," and personal prayer.[12]

The young Lutheran aristocrat, Zinzendorf, was very committed to the Lord Jesus Christ from his youth. He had completely rejected the secular pursuits of his noble contemporaries. His family wanted him to pursue law or some other field of study that would be appropriate for those in his high born position. The young Count wanted to pursue religious studies. Though born with wealth, influence, and power, Zinzendorf, found the trappings of European nobility empty and without meaning. On September 7, 1727 he married Erdmuthe Dorothea Reus, who shared his total commitment to God, the Lutheran Church, and Pietism.[13]

Though born with wealth, influence, and power, Zinzendorf, found the trappings of European nobility empty and without meaning.

Zinzendorf traced his personal relationship to Christ and his intense devotional life to one particular event that took place in1719. While on a tour of

[8] Moravian, org/history, p. 1

[9] Robert P. Gwinn, Chair, *The New Encyclopaedia Britannica, Micro. Vol. 8*, (Chicago, 1990), p. 310.

[10] Ruth A. Tucker, *From Jerusalem to Irian Jaya*, (Grand Rapids, 1983), p. 70.

[11] Ibid.

[12] Earle E. Cairns, *Christianity Through the Centuries*. (Grand Rapids, 1996), pp. 383.

[13] Robert P. Gwinn, Chair, *The New Encyclopaedia Britannica, Micro. Vol. 12*, (Chicago, 1990), p. 921.

Europe he visited an art gallery and viewed Domenico Feti's *Ecce Homo*, which was a portrait of Christ wearing the crown of thorns. The painting had an inscription that the Count said forever changed his life, "*All this I did for you, what are you doing for Me?*"[14] The nineteen year old Count was powerfully touched in a very personal way by the Holy Spirit. From that moment, Zinzendorf realized that he could never consider himself a follower of Jesus Christ and continue to live the carefree life of a European nobleman. To the horror of friends and family, he dedicated the rest of his life to the service of Jesus Christ.

Their only common ground was their love for Jesus Christ and the fact that they had all faced tremendous persecution for their beliefs.

THE MORAVIANS CONNECT WITH ZINZENDORF

The Moravians were offered sanctuary from persecution by the young nobleman on his estate at Berthelsdorf, Saxony in 1722. There they established a community of devout Christian artisans and craftsmen, which became known as Herrnhut. The word "Herrnhut" means "under the Lord's watch" or "on watch for the Lord."[15] The Moravian group was soon joined by the ragged, remnant followers of other reformers. Each group brought their own theological differences with them. Their only common ground was their love for Jesus Christ, and the fact that they had all faced tremendous persecution for their beliefs.

The Count offered these religious refugees physical protection, a place to live, and freedom to practice their devotion to God. He began to teach, organize, and influence them according to his own Pietist Lutheran training and beliefs. The people were mostly working tradesmen and the Count quickly provided the setting for them to resume working their crafts. This working fellowship of zealous followers of Christ would come to typify the Moravian movement. Ultimately, Zinzendorf developed Herrnhut into the prototype for about 20 similar communities or settlements in Europe and America. Though Zinzendorf was generally recognized as the international leader of the Moravians from 1727 until his death, he remained committed to the Lutheran Church and was actually ordained as an orthodox Lutheran pastor in 1734.[16]

THE DAY THE HOLY SPIRIT CAME TO HERRNHUT

The very zealous Moravians had found a worthy leader in Zinzendorf. He was a

[14] Tucker, p. 70.

[15] Hyatt, p. 103.

[16] Gwinn, *Britannica, Micro. Vol. 8*, p. 310.

man of serious devotion, fervent prayer, and was known for his commitment to radical holiness. In modern terminology, we would say that he had a tremendous hunger for God. The faithful believers enjoyed a respite from their centuries of persecution under his watchful eye. Collectively, the community of Herrnhut entered into what Zinzendorf termed "The Brotherly Covenant" on May 12, 1727. They mutually pledged to dedicate their lives to the service of the Lord Jesus Christ and to each other. The Moravians still adhere to the main points of this Brotherly Covenant up to the current day.[17] They developed a powerful motto that all Christians would do well to follow, *"In essentials, unity; in nonessentials, liberty; and in all things, love."*[18]

The formerly mismatched group had been growing more focused in prayer for several years. Now, they began to experience a new sense of unity. After entering into this "Brotherly Covenant" relationship with Jesus, Zinzendorf, and each other, they continued to grow more cohesive. A powerful presence of the Holy Spirit descended on Herrnhut. They began to experience this remarkable outpouring of divine favor in the summer of 1727.

During the Sunday service of August 10, 1727 the presiding pastor and the entire congregation were overwhelmed by the manifested presence of God. The pastor and every member of the gathered group fell down on the floor under the power of the Lord's mighty hand.[19] The lives of the young German Count and the Moravian Church were forever changed two days later during a communion service at Herrnhut on August 12, 1727. Descriptions of exactly what happened vary, but all accounts agree that there was a mighty visitation of the Holy Spirit. Speaking of the August 12, 1727 outpouring, Zinzendorf himself tells us:

> *A sense of the nearness of Christ was bestowed in a single moment upon all the members that were present; and it was so unanimous that two members, at work twenty miles away unaware that the meeting was being held, became at the same time deeply conscious of the same blessing.* [20]

During the Sunday service of August 10, 1727 the presiding pastor and the entire congregation were overwhelmed by the manifested presence of God.

THE HUNDRED YEAR PRAYER MEETING

The holy visitation on that remarkable summer day of 1727 did not dissipate or lift after the initial outpouring. The people of Herrnhut were overwhelmed with a

---

[17] John Greenfield, *When the Spirit Came,* (Minneapolis, 1967), p. 22.

[18] Moravian Church in America, www.moravian.org/believe/. , pp. 1.

[19] Hyatt, p. 104.

[20] Hyatt, pp. 105. Note: Hyatt is quoting from Vol. II of Zinzendorf's Journal, pp. 184-185.

God-given desire to be found constantly in prayer. People of all ages began to organize themselves into small groups to pray, day and night. On August 26, twenty-four men and twenty-four women met and covenanted together to pray twenty-four hours a day in shifts. This irresistible prayer movement continued to permeate the community as all ages pressed into the Lord's throne room in heaven. More people soon joined the initial group of forty-eight, including a number of small children. The desire to participate in this around the clock prayer watch resulted in what has been called by church historians "The Hundred Year Prayer Meeting."[21]

The Count returned home with a tremendous sense that he and the Moravian Church were to spread the gospel of Jesus Christ to the unreached people around the world.

For more than one hundred years, beginning on August 26, 1727, there was a Moravian brother or sister somewhere engaged in prayer, twenty-four hours a day, seven days a week. Among the brethren this meeting was known as the "Hourly Intercession." There was literal prayer without ceasing for one hundred years. The prayer focus soon moved from those at Herrnhut to lost souls in Europe and around the world. The Lord gave the entire community a burning desire to see sinners come to a saving knowledge of Jesus Christ and this fueled young Zinzendorf's fire for evangelism.

THE MORAVIAN MISSIONS MOVEMENT

Shortly after the mighty outpouring of the Holy Spirit and the beginning of the Hundred Year Prayer Meeting in 1727, Zinzendorf was invited to attend the coronation of Christian VI as King of Denmark. At the coronation, he met two native Greenlanders, and a black slave from the West Indies. These three people pled with him to send Christian missionaries to their countries. The Count returned home with a tremendous sense that he and the Moravian Church were to spread the gospel of Jesus Christ to the unreached people around the world.

The focus of prayer at Hernnhut became world missions. The Lord gave the entire community a renewed call of the Great Commission, to go into all the world and preach the gospel. This resulted in the greatest concentration of Christian workers being sent out into foreign missions since the first century. *"In the two decades that followed, the Moravians sent out more missionaries than all Protestants and Anglicans had sent out in the previous two centuries."*[22]

Zinzendorf spent the remaining thirty-three years of his life presiding over a worldwide network of Moravian missionaries. He instructed the faithful that they should continue their trades in the foreign lands and be self-supporting.

[21] Greenfield, pp. 24-26.

The Count set very clear guidelines for all of his foreign missionaries. They were to live humbly among the people, keep Christ as the center of their lives, and look for individual seekers as opposed to large groups of potential converts.[23] They were encouraged to start a variety of businesses, using their previous vocational skills, from shipping to baking. One writer has said that, *"The most important contribution of the Moravians, was their emphasis that every Christian is a missionary and should witness through his daily vocation."*[24]

During Zinzenforf's lifetime, one out of every sixty Moravians on earth were sent to the foreign mission field. Between 1732 and 1736, they pioneered works to the West Indies, the Virgin Islands, the Caribbean, Greenland, North America, Lapland, South America, and Africa. They later established a major outreach work in Labrador in 1771. Because of his tremendous influence, one writer has said that the Count did the most of any Christian *"to advance the cause of Protestant missions during the course of the eighteenth century"* and the same source went on to say:

> *Zinzendorf had a powerful influence on early Protestant Christianity that in many respects equaled or excelled that of his personal acquaintances, John Wesley and George Whitefield. He pioneered ecumenical evangelism, founded the Moravian church and authored scores of hymns, but above all else he launched a world-wide missionary movement that set the stage for William Carey and "The Great Century" of missions that would follow.*[25]

During Zinzenforf's lifetime, one out of every sixty Moravians on earth were sent to the foreign mission field.

JOHN WESLEY AND THE MORAVIANS

In 1734, Moravian missionaries first set foot on the shores of the American colonies in Georgia. The following year a group of their co-workers found themselves on board a ship crossing the Atlantic with two young Anglican missionaries named John and Charles Wesley. The passage was particularly difficult and at one point it appeared that the ship might go down in a storm. The young John Wesley took special note that the Moravians and their children showed no fear of death during the storm. The following account is taken from Wesley's journal entry of Sunday, January 25, 1736:

---

[22] Tucker, p. 71.

[23] Julia Davis, *The Moravian Church.*, (online paper, 1997), Pp. 3.

[24] Tucker, p. 69.

[25] Ibid. pp. 69-70.

In the midst of the psalm wherewith their service began, the sea broke over, split the mainsail in pieces, covered the ship, and poured in between the decks, as if the great deep had already swallowed us up. A terrible screaming began among the English. The Germans (Moravians) calmly sang on. I asked one of them afterward, "Were you not afraid?" He answered, "I thank God, no." I asked, "But were not your women and children afraid?" He replied, mildly, "No; our women and children are not afraid to die."[26]

This warming of his heart in the Moravian service resulted in his life becoming radically transformed into a flame of fire for his generation.

This shipboard encounter with the faithful Moravians challenged John Wesley to examine his own personal relationship with Jesus Christ. Upon arrival in Georgia he sought out the leading Moravian theologian, Bishop A.G. Spangenberg to discuss the matter further. Spangenberg asked Wesley if he knew for an absolute certainty that he was a born again child of God. The deeply challenged John Wesley told him he did; but the truth was that he had no such internal assurance. This conversation left Wesley to note in his journal, *"I went to America to convert the Indians; but oh! who shall convert me?"*[27]

After a very unsuccessful missionary trip to Georgia, John and Charles Wesley returned to England with many questions about their own relationships with Christ. They continued their association with the Moravian brothers and one of their leaders, Peter Boehler. In the following months, Boehler became quite intimate with the Wesleys and convinced them both of their need for a personal salvation experience. The brothers continued to be practicing Anglican Priests, while the Holy Spirit challenged them through the lives and theology of the Moravians.

On Wednesday, May 24, 1738, John Wesley attended a Moravian service at Aldersgate Street in London. He said that during this service his heart *"was strangely warmed."* This warming of his heart in the Moravian service resulted in his life becoming radically transformed into a flame of fire for his generation. Wesley later said the Aldersgate encounter was his personal salvation experience. John and Charles Wesley, as well as the great evangelist George Whitefield, were all powerfully influenced by the Moravians. One writer opines, *"It is not too much to say that what happened in that little meeting-house in Aldersgate Street on May 24, 1738 changed the political and religious destinies of English-speaking Protestantism."*[28]

---

[26] John Wesley, *Works of Wesley*, Vol. I, pp. 21-22.

[27] Greenfield, pp. 31-33.

THE MORAVIANS IN NORTH AMERICA

As I mentioned above, Moravian missionaries first landed in Georgia in 1734. They attempted unsuccessfully to establish a colony that could be used as a missionary base to American Indians, and a place of safe refuge if they were ever forced to flee Europe. After failing to establish a colony in Georgia, a group of the brethren settled on the estate of George Whitefield in Pennsylvania. They purchased five hundred acres from Whitefield and established the town of Bethlehem in 1741. They also purchased five thousand additional acres, including the Barony of Nazareth from Whitefield's manager. These two communities, Nazareth and Bethlehem, became the first permanent Moravian settlements and missions bases in North America. Zinzendorf himself visited the Pennsylvania settlements in 1742 and unsuccessfully attempted to unite all German Christians, including the Amish and Lutherans with the Moravians.[29]

The European leadership of the Moravians met in London on November 29, 1751 to consider the purchase of 100,000 acres of land in North Carolina from John Carteret, the Earl of Granville. They sent word to Bethlehem of their decision to buy if suitable land could be found. Bishop Spangenberg led a survey/exploration party of six brethren from Pennsylvania to North Carolina on September 18, 1752 to look for a suitable parcel of land. Between September of 1752 and January 13, 1753, they surveyed 98,985 acres of land in the colony of North Carolina. They returned to Bethlehem, Pennsylvania with their recommendations in February of 1753. In August they purchased assorted tracts in the North Carolina colony.[30]

After failing to establish a colony in Georgia, a group of the brethren settled on the estate of George Whitefield in Pennsylvania.

The property they purchased from Lord Granville included land in and around the area now known as Winston-Salem, North Carolina. The first town they established was Bethabara, followed by Bethania in the area now known as Wachovia. On February 14, 1765, they began construction of what would eventually become the city of Salem. Salem grew steadily until its borders actually joined to the growing city of Winston. The two cities consolidated and became Winston-Salem.[31]

---

[28] Greenfield, p. 36.

[29] Moravian Church in America, www.moravian.org/history., p. 2.

[30] Dallas Vogler, *The Moravians Come to North Carolina*, (Online Paper, 2003), p.1.

[31] Ibid. p.2.

The Granville land purchase also included 8,773 acres within the borders of what is now Wilkes County, North Carolina. This property contained a large section of what was to become the current city of Wilkesboro. The 8,773 acres also included Moravian Falls, which is the mountain spot that first came to my attention and sparked my interest in the Moravians. Soon after the purchase was complete, committed Christian missionaries arrived from Pennsylvania, Georgia, and Europe with a desire to pray, live holy lives, and evangelize the Indians.[32]

The Moravian Church experienced its most powerful growth and influence in the eighteenth century.

ZINZENDORF REMARRIES

Zinzendorf lost his first wife Erdmuth in 1756. The following year he married Anna Nischmann, who had formerly led the Single Sisters Choir in Bethlehem, Pennsylvania. Members of his family and social rank recoiled at the idea of the marriage. Zinzendorf was accosted for the marriage to such a degree that he kept it semi-private for almost a year. The Count had again, badly broken with his aristocratic contemporaries by marrying this American commoner.[33]

THE MORAVIAN CHURCH OF TODAY

The Moravian Church experienced its most powerful growth and influence in the eighteenth century. Today there are 418,000 confirmed communicants worldwide. In North America, there were approximately 39,000 members in 1996. Winston-Salem, North Carolina is the headquarters of their Southern Provinces and it houses a Moravian History Museum. Bethlehem, Pennsylvania is the headquarters for the Northern Provinces. Scattered pockets of the group are still found around the world in all of the major areas they evangelized in Zinzendorf's time. The highest concentration of Moravians on earth is now found in Tanzania, which accounts for 43 percent of the entire church.[34]

CONCLUSION

Only time and eternity will reveal the full extent of the impact of the Moravians on history. Clearly, their legitimate claim as the First Reformation Church has been overlooked by many historians. Their influence on John and Charles Wesley and George Whitefield is well documented and this value is inestimable. The zealous Moravian impact on the lives of these three men changed England, the United States, and Western Civilization.

---

[32] John Crouch, *Historical Sketches of Wilkes County*, (Online Paper, 1902) pp. 6.

[33] Gwinn, Britannica, Micro. Vol. 12., p. 922.

[34] Davis, p. 1.

The results of the missionary outreach efforts of Zinzendorf and his generation cannot be fully calculated.

As I have researched this subject, I have pondered the faithful Moravian missionaries to the United States and the area we now call Moravian Falls. I have come up with several possible reasons why the Lord may be continuing to pour out His blessings there. First, the area has what has been termed an "open heaven," which implies that God's voice can be clearly heard and His will clearly discerned. Deuteronomy 28:15 and 23 tell us that **"it shall come to pass, if thou wilt not hearken unto the voice of the LORD thy God,... thy heaven that is over thy head shall be brass.** Meaning, if you do not listen to God and do His will on earth, you will not have access to approach Him in prayer.

Conversely, if you do listen to God and do His will on earth, you will have access to approach Him. Clearly, the Moravians were among those who listened to God's voice, did His will, and as a result were blessed with heavenly access. The Moravians who came to North Carolina gave up everything to follow God's voice and do His will on earth. They were not subject to heavens of brass. Consequentially, they filled the atmosphere over the mountains of North Carolina with their prayers for more than one hundred years. They left Europe and came to America to serve God and preach the gospel of Jesus Christ. They gave up their lives to see His kingdom come to Moravian Falls, North Carolina and their "open heaven" can still be sensed by faithful seekers.

Second, the lasting impact of the Moravian Church around the world, and the abiding presence of God can perhaps be explained another way. In Exodus 20:24, God tells us, **"Wherever I cause my name to be honored, I will come to you and bless you" (NIV).**The names of God the Father and His Son Jesus Christ were honored in every place the Moravian missionaries went. This promise of **"I will come to you and bless you"** is not constrained by time. Perhaps the "open heaven" is a result of the Moravians having honored God's name and Him coming to bless them for it. From the martyred Reformer, John Huss, to Count Von Zinzendorf, to those who evangelized the Indians of North Carolina, Moravians have willingly abandoned their lives to follow Jesus. The blessing of God can still be felt in Moravian Falls, the mountains of North Carolina, and wherever "The Footsteps of the Moravian Church" tread the earth in the name of our Lord and Savior, Jesus Christ. ■

Clearly, the Moravians were among those who listened to God's voice, did His will, and as a result were blessed with heavenly access.

NEW FROM RICK JOYNER

Delivered from Evil

by Rick Joyner

In this third and final installment in his series on spiritual warfa Rick Joyner continues with the theme he began in *Overcoming Evil the Last Days* and *Breaking the Power of Evil. Delivered from E* tackles the strongholds of fear, confusion, and human idealism.

Before the end of this age, there will be a generation that walks love, truth, righteousness, and true spiritual authority. In Deliver from Evil, Rick Joyner offers practical wisdom and insight that w help you take your place in this mighty generation that will prevail ov the gross darkness of our times.

Softcover, Item # RJ1-045 Retail $13.95
Our Price $12.00

•NEW BOOKS FROM MORNINGSTAR•

The Apostolic Ministry

by Rick Joyner

The ministry of the apostle is the linchpin ministry of the church. Without it the church cannot become what it is called to be. Rick answers key questions in *The Apostolic Ministry* concerning one of the important subjects of our time.

Softcover, 184 pgs. Item # RJ1-044 Retail $14.95
Our Price $12.00

Father: A Look Into the Heart of God

by Geri Keller

"Geri's special relationship to the Father is apparent to all who know him. I know of no other person more qualified to write this book than Geri, and he has done it masterfully." —*Rick Joyner*

Softcover, 199 pgs. Item # GK1-001 Retail $14.95
Our Price $12.00

Power Points from the Word: A 52-Week Devotional

by Andrew P. Surace

"Usually when I read a manuscript, I think what the author has written into a book should really have been written as a short article. *With Power Points from the Word,* I felt that almost every chapter of this work could have been a book." —*Rick Joyner*

Softcover, 124 pgs. Item # AS1-001 Retail $9.95
Our Price $8.00

10 Pillars of Christian Leadership

by Dr. John ChaCha

"Dr. ChaCha does more than jus instruct in his teaching, he imparts wisdom and builds faith. This book will help you to become what God has called you to be." —*Rick Joyner*

Softcover, 139 pgs. Item # JC2-001 Retail $9.95
Our Price $8.00

To order call 1-800-542-0278

[Equipping the Saints for the Work of Ministry]
MorningStar
FELLOWSHIP CHURCH

Statement of Ownership, Management, and Circulation

(Required by 39 U.S.C. 3685)

1. Publication Title: The Morning Star Journal® 2. Publication No.: 0129-03
3. Filing Date: October 1, 2004 4. Issue frequency: Quarterly
5. No. of issues published annually: 4 6. Annual Subscription Price: $16.95 U.S.; $24.95 Int'l
7. Complete Mailing Address of Known Office of Publication: 1605 Industrial Drive., Wilkesboro, NC 28697
   Contact person: David Hart, Telephone: 336-651-2400, ext. 105
8. Complete Mailing Address of General Office of Publisher: same as #7
9. Publisher: MorningStar Publications, P.O. Box 440, Wilkesboro, NC 28697
   Editor: Rick Joyner, P.O. Box 440, Wilkesboro, NC 28697
   Managing Editor: Deborah Joyner Johnson, P.O. Box 440, Wilkesboro, NC 28697
10. Owner: MorningStar Fellowship Church, P.O. Box 440, Wilkesboro, NC 28697
11. There are no Bondholders, Mortgagees, or Other Security Holders.
12. The purpose, function, and nonprofit status of this organization and the exempt status for federal income tax purposes has not changed during the preceding 12 months.

13. Publication Title: The Morning Star Journal® 14. Issue Date of Circulation Date Below: October 2003 15. Extent and Nature of Circulation	Average No. Copies Each Issue During Preceding 12 Months	No. Copies of Single Issue Published Nearest to Filing Date
a. Total No. of Copies (Net Press Run)	20,000	20,000
b. Paid and/or Requested Circulation		
(1) Paid/Requested Outside-County Mail Subscriptions	10,961	10,382
(2) Paid In-County Subscriptions	12	12
(3) Sales Through Dealers and Carriers, Street Vendors, and Counter Sales, and Other Non-USPS Paid Distribution	107	96
(4) Other Classes Mailed Through the USPS00		
c. Total Paid and/or Requested Circulation	11,080	10,490
d. Free Distribution by Mail		
(1) Outside-County	0	0
(2) In-County	0	0
(3) Other Classes Mailed Through the USPS	0	0
e. Free Distribution Outside the Mail	84	84
f. Total Free Distribution	84	84
g. Total Distribution	11,164	10,574
h. Copies Not Distributed	8,836	9,426
i. Total Sum of 15g. and h.)	20,000	20,000
j. Percent Paid and/or Requested Circulation	99%	99%

16. This Statement of Ownership will be printed in the Vol.14-4 issue of this publication.

David Hart, Office Business Manager, August 26, 2004